More Literature Puzzles for Elementary and Middle Schools

MORE
LITERATURE PUZZLES
for
Elementary and Middle Schools

CAROL J. VEITCH
and
JANE E. CRAWFORD

Illustrated by
Patricia A. Mannerberg

LIBRARIES UNLIMITED, INC.
Littleton, Colorado

1986

LIBRARIES UNLIMITED, INC.
P.O. Box 263
Littleton. Colorado 80160-0263

Library of Congress Cataloging-in-Publication Data

Veitch, Carol J., 1942-
    More literature puzzles for elementary and middle
schools.

    Bibliography: p. 89
    Includes indexes.
    1. Literary recreations. 2. Crossword puzzles.
3. Word games. 4. Educational games. I. Crawford,
Jane E., 1938-   . II. Title.
GV1493.V443 1986   793.73   86-7161
ISBN 0-87287-518-0

Libraries Unlimited books are bound with Type II nonwoven material that meets and exceeds
National Association of State Textbook Administrators' Type II nonwoven material specifications
Class A through E.

To all our loved ones with thanks.

TABLE OF CONTENTS

PUZZLES

ANSWERS

INDEXES

BIBLIOGRAPHY

PREFACE

More Literature Puzzles for Elementary and Middle Schools, like its predecessor, *Literature Puzzles for Elementary and Middle Schools*, has been designed to supplement the upper elementary, middle, or junior high school literature program by providing enrichment activities in the form of seek-a-word and crossword puzzles for twenty-five popular titles. Titles selected for this puzzle book come from a wide range of literary genres and readability levels. Newbery Award winners and runners-up are well represented. The authors have made a conscious effort to include titles which would be widely available in most library collections serving grades 4-8.

The words and illustrations for each of the seek-a-word puzzles have been chosen from the individual book's incidents or characters. The puzzle will help students who have read the book recall these characters and events. For students who have not read a particular book, the puzzle can be used to arouse interest as the words suggest interesting events in the book.

The crossword puzzles have been developed to reinforce the student's memory of incidents and characters in each book; the clues relate directly to these. For this reason, the crossword puzzles probably will not be successful with students who have not read the book to which the puzzle relates.

Puzzles in *More Literature Puzzles for Elementary and Middle Schools* can be used equally well by classroom teachers, school librarians, and children's or young adult public librarians for individual students or groups of students. The puzzles can be used in a variety of ways.

1. Puzzles might serve as a whole-class activity after the teacher or librarian has read the book to the class or after the class has studied the book in the literature program.

2. In an activity center in the library or classroom, individual students could work the puzzles as they chose. Puzzle pages could either be duplicated or laminated. A transparency of the puzzle page with answers marked would enable a student to check his or her answers quickly. Posting a laminated answer sheet near the activity center would also allow the student to check answers easily and independently. Displaying the book(s) in the center would serve as a further enticement to read or reread the book(s).

3. Public and school librarians could duplicate puzzle pages to distribute to library users in conjunction with summer reading programs or to promote other special reading activities or events.

4. The crossword puzzles might serve as an alternative for the traditional book report, as the student would have to read the book before he or she could do the puzzle.

5. Puzzles, especially the seek-a-word puzzles, could be used as a special treat before holidays or other times when a break in the routine is desirable.

6. Younger students can color in the illustrations after they have worked a seek-a-word puzzle.

7. Puzzles are effective and enjoyable devices for teaching problem-solving techniques, thus reinforcing other curricular objectives. The seek-a-word puzzles are especially effective for developing search strategies, helping students see letter patterns within words, and challenging students to find words hidden in the puzzles.

8. Crossword puzzles are especially effective for developing recall of specific events and characters in the books, increasing vocabulary, and using word recognition skills to help fill in puzzle blanks.

9. The puzzles could serve as a springboard to student-designed puzzles for other books which the students have enjoyed reading and would like to share in this way with classmates. Use of computer programs for puzzle design, e.g., CROSSWORD MAGIC (Mindscape, Inc.) would enhance the student's use of the computer in a different game situation. The puzzles in *Literature Puzzles for Elementary and Middle Schools* and *More Literature Puzzles for Elementary and Middle Schools* could be used as examples of literature-based puzzles. The designing of puzzles is creative and forces students to think about books in terms of important characters and events as students choose the words and clues for their own puzzles. Puzzle-making might easily substitute for the traditional book report, since students would have to read the book carefully before a puzzle could be developed effectively.

This book includes both a crossword and a seek-a-word puzzle for each title. Crossword puzzles for *More Literature Puzzles for Elementary and Middle Schools* were designed on an Apple II+ using CROSSWORD MAGIC developed by L & S Computerware for Mindscape, Inc. All illustrations for the seek-a-word puzzles were drawn by Pat Mannerberg; she and Jane Crawford share the credit for crossword puzzle art. Answers to the puzzles appear at the back of the book, and Jane deserves all the credit for that tedious work.

The suggested grade-level index is intended only as a guide for titles which might not be familiar to persons using this puzzle book. The grade-level index is in no way intended to limit the use of any puzzle. Many of the titles can be used with gifted students or voracious readers in grades lower than those suggested, while slower students or reluctant readers in upper grades might find some of the easier titles appealing. As with all materials, the teacher or librarian must be guided by his or her knowledge of the particular book and the interests of the individual student or class. For the purposes of this puzzle book, the grade-level designations were developed from my experience as a middle school librarian and from consultation with other librarians and classroom teachers. Puzzle difficulty was, to some degree, geared to those grade-level suggestions.

All of the suggestions for using *More Literature Puzzles for Elementary and Middle Schools* are designed to get the user started thinking about ways to use the books and puzzles with students. They are only starting points. ENJOY!!!

Carol J. Veitch

ACKNOWLEDGMENTS

No book just happens. Many people besides the authors and illustrator play important roles in the creation of a book. We would like to take this opportunity to publicly thank some of these special people.

Patsy Casey, librarian at Currituck County High School, Barco, N.C., for the use of her printer.

Robert L. Ford, Drafting and Design Department, College of the Albemarle, Elizabeth City, N.C., for his advice.

Anne D. Sanders, Alise Irvin, and the staffs of the East Albemarle Regional Libraries, Elizabeth City, N.C., for their varied support and assistance.

Heather Cameron, editor at Libraries Unlimited, for her patience and support.

All the folks at Engineering Media, Chesapeake, Va., for their assistance.

Our families and friends for their interest and encouragement.

PUZZLES

The Best Christmas Pageant Ever

By Barbara Robinson

SEEK-A-WORD

```
C O S T U M E P D H C E F B R
H A Z A S O U K C E T S I R E
R Q T R A H T R N A M D R E H
I H O G L M U E I R B Q E A E
S L F E G H S G Z E H Y M C A
T A G R C S T E R C E S R L R
M N E U E A F D R E H P E H S
A S T R N L I C E I L D A H A
S W R I E I G R Y R A R B I L
N S O B M O M D F E T A E M A
R T U A E L D N A C B P H O E
Y S B T S E T E D Y M E E G S
M A L C I N I G N U R H R E C
A T E P W O N D E R N S L N H
P A G E A N T A H S E M C E S
```

WORDS:

Angel
Baby
Candle
Cat
Christmas
Church
Costume
Fire
Gifts
Ham

Herdman
Imogene
Library
Pageant
Rehearsal
Secrets
Shepherd
Trouble
Wisemen
Wonder

The Best Christmas Pageant Ever

By Barbara Robinson

CROSSWORD

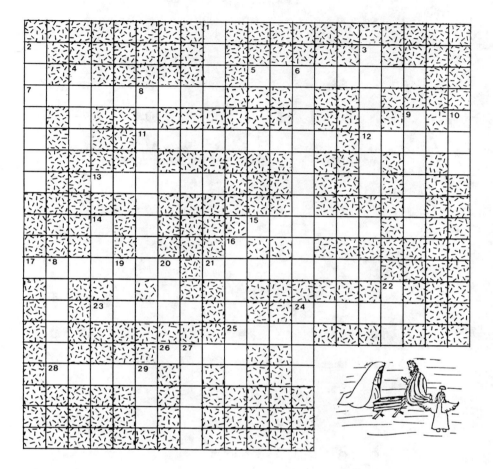

ACROSS

5. The _____ burned Fred Shoemaker's toolhouse.
7. _____ cloths, used long ago to wrap a baby.
11. The shepherds wore _____.
12. _____ thought she should be Mary.
13. _____, the meanest Herdman of all.
15. Gladys slept in a _____ when she was a baby.
17. _____ blackmailed the fat kids.
21. Reverend Hopkins was the _____.
23. _____ came to Imogene's eyes.
24. Imogene _____ the baby Jesus.
25. The potluck committee burned the applesauce _____.
26. Everyone _____ to see the Herdmans.
28. _____ played Joseph.

DOWN

1. The Herdmans wanted to _____ King Herod.
2. Leroy, Claude, and Ollie were the _____.
3. The Herdmans took over the _____.
4. Pennies were stolen from the Happy Birthday _____.
6. _____ were hectic!
8. Miss Graebher was the _____.
9. Imogene smoked _____.
10. "_____! Unto you a child is born."
14. Mrs. Armstrong broke her _____.
16. Gladys _____ Imogene's ears.
18. "Away in a _____."
19. The Herdman's cat had one missing _____.
20. A pussy willow sprouted in Ollie's _____.
22. Christmas was given a _____ meaning.
24. The pageant was the _____ ever.
27. An _____ named the baby "Jesus."
29. The wise men brought _____ as their gifts.

The Black Pearl

By Scott O'Dell

SEEK-A-WORD

```
L  N  A  B  S  N  A  I  D  N  I  E  S  H  M
A  S  L  L  E  H  S  L  E  O  S  H  F  A  A
A  R  I  A  O  S  H  O  K  E  W  A  D  L  N
F  N  A  V  N  I  L  C  A  K  L  O  Q  R  T
A  T  E  E  L  F  A  S  E  H  N  V  N  S  A
N  Z  R  A  O  L  N  I  O  N  A  I  E  P  D
O  F  D  K  B  I  T  D  A  E  R  O  F  N  I
O  A  T  S  E  V  I  L  L  A  N  O  R  E  A
G  E  L  C  O  E  A  O  E  A  S  C  A  N  B
A  N  T  E  A  D  P  I  C  O  P  S  E  A  L
L  O  A  F  I  E  S  T  A  F  L  A  L  D  O
N  M  N  V  N  O  D  I  V  R  A  B  Z  I  N
I  A  E  L  S  E  A  M  A  L  E  U  P  K  L
G  R  A  V  I  L  C  E  S  M  I  H  E  F  B
C  E  M  N  O  O  P  R  A  H  D  C  A  V  E
```

WORDS:

Black	Knife
Cave	Lagoon
Canoe	La Paz
Chubasco	Madonna
Devilfish	Manta Diablo
Diver	Pearl
Fiesta	Ramon
Fleet	Sea
Harpoon	Sevillano
Indians	Shells

The Black Pearl
By Scott O'Dell

CROSSWORD

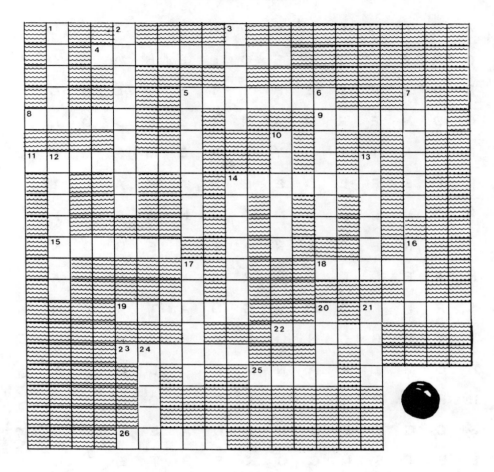

ACROSS

4. _____ Sea.
5. Los _____, the Island of the Dead.
8. The Salazar family were _____ dealers.
9. Soto Luzon was an _____.
11. A dreaded tropical wind.
14. Santa _____, one of the ships in the Salazar fleet.
15. Pearls are found in _____ shells.
18. _____ Diablo.
19. The Great Pearl weighed 62.3 _____.
21. Color of the Great Pearl.
22. Central square of Mexican towns.
23. The village _____, Father Gallardo.
25. Number of boats in the Salazar fleet.
26. Ramon's grandfather gave him a _____.

DOWN

1. Ramon _____ the pearl from the church.
2. Gaspar Ruiz's nickname.
3. Ramon wanted to become a _____.
5. The _____, the Lady of the Sea.
6. Ramon's age.
7. Type of oar used with a canoe.
10. Party or feast.
12. Ruiz tried to _____ the giant manta.
13. A shallow lake connected to the sea.
14. There were many _____ on the Island of the Dead.
16. _____ California.
17. The Pearl of _____.
20. The giant manta lived in a _____.
21. Mantas are shaped like giant _____.
24. _____ Salazar.

The Borrowers

By Mary Norton

SEEK-A-WORD

```
P A H O M L L N D B O T T L E
B O R A I Y I E O L E H A N G
B R D R R P E P T T S U E B G
T O O V E R M A N T L E S O L
O H Y I T T I Y A N E M N M E
R R I S E L D E E N A R A I T
S P D M E E D M T S N B E G I
R I I N B C Y R A T Y E B O N
E N A E L L I E R A Y R N T A
W S R I I O E V G M A T A T H
O T Y M B C N O I P B E M N O
R H O M L K A N M E E L U T A
R H R E P E E K E S U O H U U
O E G G E E S L C U A E N S E
B L E T S N C O K E P T E E K
```

WORDS:

Arrietty	Housekeeper
Aunt	Human bean
Borrowers	Letter
Bottle	Needles
Boy	Overmantles
Clock	Pin
Diary	Pod
Eggletina	Seen
Emigrate	Stamp
Homily	Thimble

The Borrowers

By Mary Norton

CROSSWORD

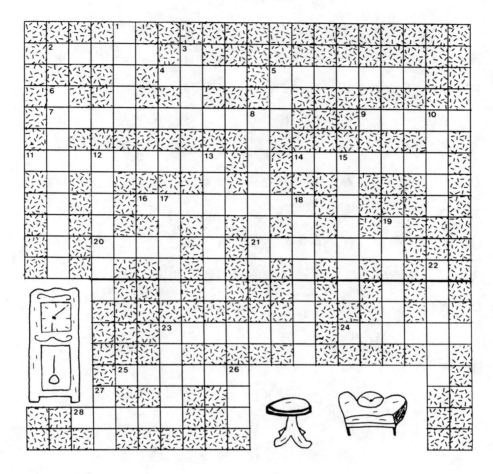

ACROSS

2. Mrs. May and Kate were making a _____.
4. Human _____.
5. The boy used a pickax to open the _____.
7. The _____ lived behind the mantlepiece.
9. Pod's last name.
11. The gardener.
14. Breakfast was served in the _____ room.
16. Portraits of Queen _____ hung on the walls.
20. Arrietty _____ to the boy.
21. The ratcatcher's dog.
23. Fibers from the _____ made a brush.
24. The housekeeper was _____ of mice/the Borrowers.
25. The _____ was made from an oak apple.
28. Great Aunt _____.

DOWN

1. Homily wanted a parquet _____.
3. Pod was "_____" by the boy.
5. The _____ pipe.
6. Mrs. May told Kate about the _____.
8. The Borrowers had to _____.
10. The _____ box had a lid with ladies on it.
12. "She" drank fine old pale _____.
13. The walls were papered with old _____.
15. _____ was important to the Borrowers so they would know where people were.
17. Where the boy lived before he came to his aunt's.
18. The youngest Borrower.
19. Mrs. _____ was the housekeeper.
22. _____ was the mother.
23. Mrs. May found Arrietty's _____.
26. English meal. (Hint: This is also a drink.)
27. _____ Thumb Gazetteer of the World.

The Cabin Faced West

By Jean Fritz

SEEK-A-WORD

```
V R S T E N C E R E T I S I V
O E I W U R A G N O Q U T M B
T H G N O T B E A S M G W P T
E T W A S H I N G T O N A O E
S R D Y T R N S L E T T E R R
T G V H I A Y R S G A S E T U
M T O E E T B Q A C U T B A T
E U C L N U R L I A H L G N U
G R U B S Y T T E G I U P T F
A R A E I T P R U S E L R A S
R T P Y M O U A F M T G V C N
U B S E T A L P R A L O R A H
O I H S R N D O E T A D E O L
C R E L G I T R L H Y R A I D
A W T C O S E L B A T E G E V
```

WORDS:

Ann	Logs
Cabin	Party
Church	Plates
Courage	Road
Diary	Rule
Future	Storm
Gettysburg	Vegetables
Important	Visit
Laughter	Washington
Letter	West

The Cabin Faced West

By Jean Fritz

CROSSWORD

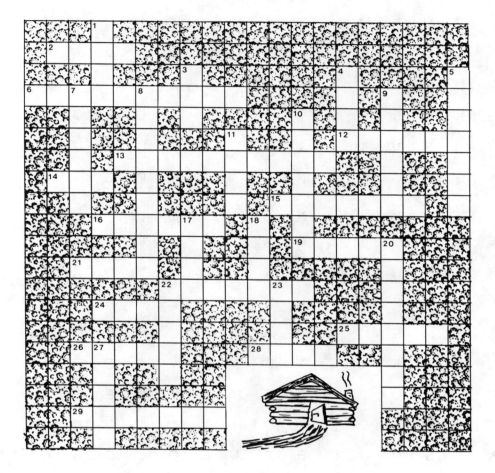

ACROSS

2. A street or highway.
6. Where the Hamiltons once lived.
12. Margaret sent Ann a _____.
13. George _____.
14. Ann and her mother had a _____ party on Hamilton Hill.
15. Deer meat.
16. _____ cake.
19. A fierce _____ destroyed the vegetable garden.
21. Color of Ann's shoes.
22. _____ Country (where Ann lived).
24. Ann's _____ ribbons were blue.
25. Ann kept a _____.
26. Ann married Arthur _____ when she grew up.
28. Vegetable which is shelled.
29. There were no _____ in the cabin.

DOWN

1. Old fashioned word for eat.
3. "My _____ runneth over."
4. David threw a _____ of cold water on Daniel.
5. Bravery.
7. Andy shot a _____ with his slingshot.
8. Name of Ann's doll.
9. Vegetable which grows underground.
10. The china plates had lavender _____.
11. _____ McPhail.
17. "Put your _____ in the pot."
18. A tinderbox was used to start a _____.
20. _____ was Ann's cousin.
22. Ann taught Andy to _____.
23. Daniel made a _____ about complaining.
27. A log _____.

Chitty Chitty Bang Bang

By Ian Fleming

SEEK-A-WORD

```
J  E  M  I  M  A  M  I  M  R  E  G  N  A  D
E  S  O  J  E  R  E  N  F  O  T  O  M  A  Y
R  D  T  M  Y  J  E  C  R  R  I  T  N  A  N
E  K  O  S  R  E  T  S  G  N  A  G  I  O  A
M  R  R  V  R  A  T  O  V  O  E  N  A  U  M
Y  B  C  G  E  R  N  E  B  R  M  P  C  S  I
D  L  A  U  R  R  S  D  E  P  S  U  H  E  T
E  A  R  N  E  C  E  R  E  R  O  L  P  X  E
P  C  D  B  G  E  I  N  V  E  N  T  O  R  C
P  I  O  P  P  C  H  H  I  G  L  R  A  H  X
A  G  M  S  K  R  U  M  S  H  U  S  I  N  Y
N  A  A  S  K  T  T  D  E  Y  Y  T  C  E  D
D  M  K  D  T  N  A  P  P  M  T  T  E  O  N
I  S  K  E  L  E  T  O  N  Y  L  C  O  N  A
K  T  S  N  G  S  E  T  A  L  O  C  O  H  C
```

WORDS:

Bang	Green
Candy	Inventor
Chitty	Jemima
Chocolates	Jeremy
Danger	Kidnapped
Dover	Magical
Dynamite	Motorcar
Explorer	Skeleton
France	Skrumshus
Gangsters	Speedboat

Chitty Chitty Bang Bang

By Ian Fleming

CROSSWORD

ACROSS

2. Paragon _____.
4. A knob on the dashboard said, "Pull _____!"
6. The _____ was a lightship.
9. Monsieur _____.
10. Mrs. Pott's first name.
11. _____ Limited, the candy factory.
15. Not mile, but _____.
17. Ships, racing cars, and airplanes are called "_____."
18. French money unit.
19. The horn was shaped like a _____ constrictor.
21. Mr. Pott was an explorer and an _____.
23. Chitty headed across the English _____ to France.
24. Madame gave the Pott family her recipe for _____.
26. Heavy mist.
27. The license plate could have read "_____."
28. Mr. Pott had been a _____ commander.

DOWN

1. Transmogrifications are _____.
3. English money unit.
5. Mr. Pott paid fifty pounds for _____.
7. Crackpot _____ sweets.
8. Joe the _____.
12. Right in naval terms.
13. Jeremy and Jemima were _____.
14. The Pott family found a _____ hanging in the cave.
16. Chitty was a _____ car.
19. Mice with wings.
20. A flying car or _____.
22. Jeremy found a cave at the base of a _____.
24. Man-Mountain _____.
25. Color of the car.

The Door in the Wall

By Marguerite De Angeli

SEEK-A-WORD

```
B  K  R  Q  S  K  R  A  M  T  S  R  C  E  W
A  T  E  V  P  N  O  W  E  R  I  P  T  N  J
O  E  L  T  T  A  B  U  R  C  S  E  A  E  L
U  S  T  B  L  E  I  Y  H  R  K  F  N  M  F
N  M  T  R  M  O  N  K  S  U  A  Z  E  Y  I
R  S  I  P  K  T  O  B  L  T  M  R  H  U  S
A  E  H  Q  M  L  G  R  E  C  T  S  E  T  H
W  B  W  R  H  T  E  S  O  H  A  R  P  Q  I
D  S  W  E  L  H  N  L  N  E  O  L  H  A  N
O  R  G  A  T  G  A  R  K  S  W  I  M  T  G
H  E  R  O  H  I  C  E  D  T  A  H  T  O  D
C  B  R  I  E  N  A  G  W  N  L  I  R  M  R
R  B  C  L  I  K  T  N  I  E  L  T  S  A  C
F  O  G  D  M  S  O  A  L  F  S  H  O  I  M
B  R  E  S  A  W  F  D  O  O  R  E  B  T  W
```

WORDS:

Battle
Brother Luke
Castle
Crutches
Danger
Door
Enemy
Fishing
Fog
Harp

Hero
Knight
Monk
Robbers
Robin
St. Marks
Swim
Wall
Warn
Whittle

The Door in the Wall

By Marguerite De Angeli

CROSSWORD

ACROSS

1. A serious disease.
6. A flat cake.
7. Sir Hugh's men ended the _____ at Lindsay.
10. A stringed musical instrument.
12. Sheepskin writing surface.
15. Robin's father was fighting the _____.
16. _____ porridge.
18. Geoffrey called Robin a "_____."
19. "Duck on a Rock" is a _____.
20. To carve something from wood.
22. Robin thought _____ would be as much fun as stilts.
23. Robbers.
25. Robin's _____ were crippled.
26. Robin went swimming in the _____.
27. John-Go-in-the-_____.
28. At the monastery Robin learned to _____ and write.

DOWN

2. Village where Sir Peter lived.
3. Robin's father was a _____.
4. A heavy mist.
5. The dog who became Robin's friend.
8. Robin was reunited with his parents on Christmas _____.
9. A "_____ and Judy" show.
11. Brother _____ was a carpenter.
13. Where the monks lived.
14. St. _____.
17. _____ Luke.
21. The _____ attacked the castle at Lindsay.
24. A jennet, or a Spanish _____.
25. A _____-in-waiting.
27. The door in the _____.

The Great Gilly Hopkins

By Katherine Paterson

SEEK-A-WORD

```
B  R  I  G  A  L  A  D  R  I  E  L  I  W  D
F  L  U  X  Q  R  B  L  O  Y  E  K  R  U  T
A  L  I  E  O  D  W  Y  D  F  I  E  N  D  F
T  C  A  N  L  A  R  E  O  T  H  G  I  F  O
F  L  T  Y  D  T  L  N  I  T  E  O  L  E  S
T  E  A  N  E  R  E  O  O  G  M  R  U  I  T
A  W  I  L  L  I  A  M  E  R  N  E  S  T  E
Y  E  T  A  H  E  N  T  H  I  R  D  V  N  R
R  L  N  D  L  G  R  S  E  A  W  R  E  A  D
E  F  I  D  E  N  A  L  P  R  I  A  T  R  K
T  A  U  E  L  I  F  D  A  E  D  C  Q  O  E
T  R  O  R  A  X  G  S  O  M  V  T  E  X  L
O  E  L  T  L  O  I  L  A  E  T  S  M  R  P
R  S  I  F  E  B  P  T  M  A  L  O  V  E  W
T  B  O  M  R  R  A  N  D  O  L  P  H  G  R
```

WORDS:

Airplane	Money
Blind	Mother
Boxing	Mr. Randolph
Fight	Postcard
Flu	Read
Foster	Steal
Galadriel	Trotter
Ladder	Turkey
Lie	Welfare
Love	William Ernest

The Great Gilly Hopkins

By Katherine Paterson

CROSSWORD

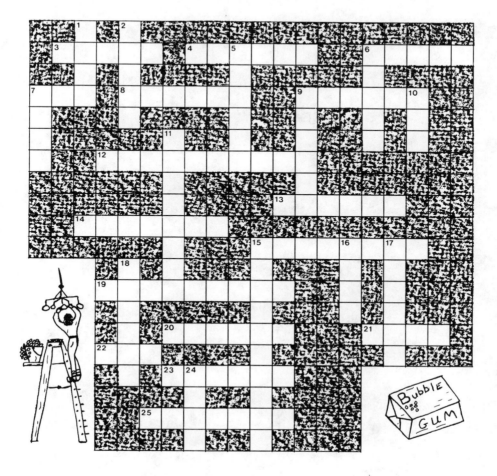

ACROSS

3. Courtney came to _____ at Christmas.
4. The _____ *Book of English Verse.*
6. Mrs. Hopkins drove a _____.
7. Gilly tried to buy a _____ ticket to San Francisco.
8. Miss _____, Gilly's teacher.
9. Miss Ellis was a _____ worker.
12. Gilly's mother lived in _____ (state).
13. Gilly sent her mother a _____.
14. Courtney picked Gilly's name from a book by _____.
15. Taking other people's money is _____.
19. Gilly's real name.
20. _____ gum.
21. At Thanksgiving everyone except Gilly got _____.
22. Color of Agnes Stokes's hair.
23. "... trailing _____ of glory."
25. Maime _____ was a foster mother.

DOWN

1. Melvin Trotter wore wild _____.
2. Gilly taught W.E. to _____ back.
5. Gilly lived in three different _____ homes.
6. Mr. Randolph was the _____ man who lived next door to Trotter.
7. Where Mr. Randolph hid some money.
9. William Ernest's favorite TV show was "_____ Street."
10. A falsehood.
11. Gilly's grandmother lived in _____ (state).
15. Gilly climbed the _____ to clean the chandelier.
16. "I _____ you," Gilly told Trotter.
17. Gilly called her grandmother _____.
18. Mr. Randolph's son was a _____.
24. Agnes acted as _____out for Gilly.

Harriet the Spy

By Louise Fitzhugh

SEEK-A-WORD

```
G  Q  S  I  N  S  P  O  E  R  O  M  E  L  X
A  R  S  S  Y  L  L  O  G  E  L  O  T  P  S
T  L  E  E  M  E  O  W  G  R  E  B  S  T  P
O  E  G  G  C  R  E  A  M  I  G  W  P  M  K
R  A  I  G  O  R  S  J  Q  T  E  A  E  Q  O
E  Z  H  R  O  R  E  E  A  A  O  M  C  S  O
T  G  G  C  R  I  Y  T  T  N  P  M  T  T  B
I  Q  U  A  H  A  L  S  S  U  I  J  A  R  E
A  R  H  U  M  E  H  Q  C  I  O  E  C  T  T
W  A  Z  G  T  I  M  Z  A  H  I  R  L  S  O
B  R  T  H  R  R  Q  I  T  S  O  R  E  O  N
M  M  I  T  T  R  O  P  S  N  T  O  S  T  O
U  S  F  T  R  I  E  T  I  T  E  Y  L  P  I
D  L  E  O  E  O  T  O  I  O  R  S  Y  S  Y
E  D  I  T  O  R  N  G  G  C  R  Y  P  R  Q
```

WORDS:

Caught

Chemistry

Dumbwaiter

Editor

Egg cream

Fitzhugh

Gregory School

Harriet

Janie

Notebook

Ole Golly

Onion

Route

Secrets

Spectacles

Sport

Spy

Sweatshirt

Tomato

Writer

Harriet the Spy

By Louise Fitzhugh

CROSSWORD

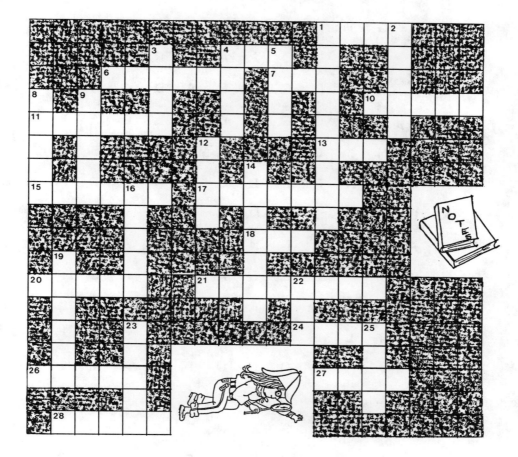

ACROSS

1. Harrison Withers had twenty-six _____.
4. Mrs. Golly was very _____.
6. Harriet wanted to be a _____.
7. _____ Golly, the governess.
10. The DeiSanti family owned a _____ store.
11. The boy with the _____ socks.
13. Harriet had a regular _____ route.
15. "There is nothing like a good _____ sandwich."
17. _____ School.
18. Dr. Wagner had _____ hair.
20. The black-rimmed spectacles had no _____ in them.
21. Harriet wrote her thoughts in this.
24. _____ waiter.
26. Harriet was an _____ in the Christmas play.
27. The Spy Catcher _____.
28. Beth _____ was very shy.

DOWN

1. Janie Gibbs had a _____ set.
2. Miss Elsor taught _____ grade.
3. Mr. Waldenstein had a delivery _____.
4. Harriet put a _____ in Marion's desk.
5. Game Harriet played.
8. _____ wanted to be a baseball player.
9. Egg _____.
12. "... and whether _____ have wings."
14. "The book is going to be called _____ by Harriet M. Welch."
16. Harriet carried her _____ on her belt.
19. Harriet's age.
22. Agatha Plumber stayed in _____ all day.
23. _____ threw a spitball at Harriet.
25. _____ jeans.

17

The Incredible Journey

By Sheila Burnford

SEEK-A-WORD

```
A  D  I  G  T  H  N  C  H  I  L  D  R  E  N
P  Y  E  N  R  U  O  J  A  T  R  Q  K  I  U
N  R  N  I  R  N  R  O  P  A  D  A  N  A  C
W  O  K  T  E  G  E  H  D  N  L  E  A  Y  N
I  D  R  N  I  E  A  N  R  E  V  D  E  W  S
L  A  E  U  R  R  E  L  U  E  N  N  R  I  R
D  R  I  H  R  S  D  O  G  A  D  I  D  N  E
E  B  A  R  E  A  I  N  L  R  T  A  F  C  L
R  A  G  M  T  B  L  G  A  E  H  R  E  T  E
N  L  A  N  L  E  N  R  R  I  L  X  I  L  V
E  I  D  T  L  E  L  I  H  Z  C  R  I  G  A
S  Q  I  J  U  L  O  D  U  I  N  A  M  E  R
S  A  K  L  B  X  C  G  T  L  R  E  B  S  T
I  N  D  I  A  N  S  E  N  T  E  U  H  I  C
C  X  E  L  B  I  D  E  R  C  N  I  E  B  N
```

WORDS:

Bull terrier

Cabin

Canada

Children

England

Excited

Hunger

Hunting

Incredible

Indians

John Longridge

Journey

Labrador

Lake

Leader

Siamese

Trail

Travelers

Wilderness

Writer

The Incredible Journey

By Sheila Burnford

CROSSWORD

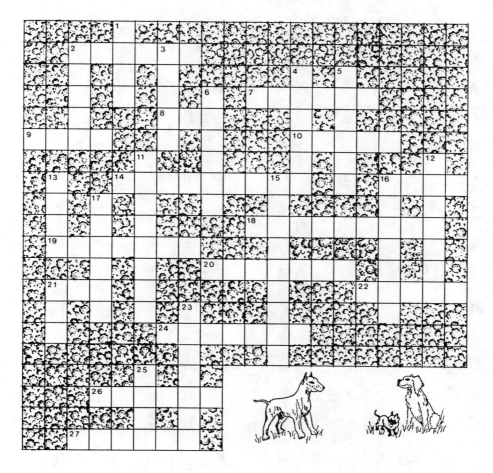

ACROSS

2. Tao nearly _____ Elizabeth when he returned.
7. There were _____, and howls, and laughter when the trio returned.
8. Elizabeth's cat's name.
9. Tao was trapped in a rabbit burrow by a _____.
10. _____ was the Labrador's name.
14. Mr. _____ removed the quills from Luath's face.
16. Helvi placed Tao in the _____ to get warm.
18. The sound of a baby's cry was only a _____.
19. _____, homeland of the Nurmi family.
20. The cat was a _____.
21. Elizabeth brought her cat a _____ collar from England.
22. Mr. and Mrs. _____ looked after the house and garden.
24. The dogs were run off with shotgun _____.
26. John Longridge was a _____.
27. Luath had porcupine _____ in his cheek.

DOWN

1. Part of the _____ landed in the fireplace.
2. An old man took the dogs into his _____.
3. Mrs. Oakes found the house _____ when she arrived.
4. Bodger and Luath tangled with a _____ dog after their chicken dinner.
5. Tao saved Bodger from a bear _____.
6. Peter's dog's name.
11. One dog was a bull terrier, the other a _____.
12. The last fifty miles of the journey were through the Strellon Game _____.
13. Tao became temporarily _____ from his ordeal in the river.
15. The trio traveled across country over the _____ Range.
16. Name of an Indian tribe.
17. The journey took place in _____.
21. The old dog collapsed in a _____.
23. The _____ dam had been in the river.
25. Helvi was the _____ who rescued Tao from the river.

19

It's Not the End of the World

By Judy Blume

SEEK-A-WORD

```
O  G  J  F  E  T  D  R  S  V  D  L  R  O  W
E  I  P  L  I  O  N  I  C  R  E  A  N  M  E
A  E  Y  K  A  R  E  N  H  W  T  W  A  I  D
G  R  B  O  S  L  Y  H  O  Q  D  Y  L  J  W
D  I  V  O  R  C  E  R  O  M  C  E  K  I  F
E  J  O  B  E  S  M  E  L  B  O  R  P  M  F
S  K  E  Y  L  O  A  C  I  R  L  H  A  T  E
S  W  D  A  P  A  R  T  M  E  N  T  K  L  J
E  T  W  D  O  B  R  E  F  C  O  U  E  O  F
R  D  S  N  V  E  I  R  L  N  S  R  A  P  Q
T  E  H  T  F  O  A  T  K  R  F  I  G  H  T
D  V  I  K  I  N  G  S  A  G  B  O  N  C  L
A  O  A  B  J  O  E  D  Q  R  E  K  Y  D  U
E  M  E  W  F  A  L  M  O  V  W  M  P  S  A
W  S  L  K  H  S  N  I  S  D  N  E  I  R  F
```

WORDS:

Apartment
Day book
Dessert
Divorce
End
Fault
Fight
Friends
Hate
Jeff

Job
Karen
Lawyer
Marriage
Mew
Move
Problems
School
Vikings
World

20

It's Not the End of the World
By Judy Blume

CROSSWORD

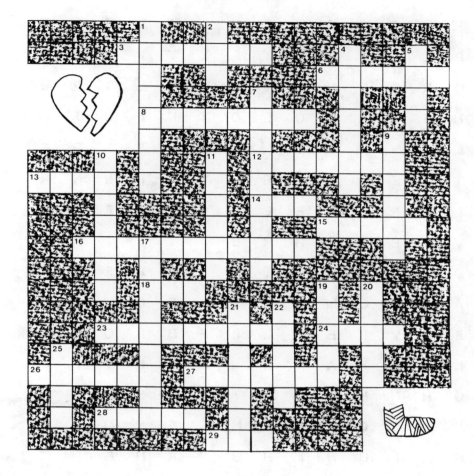

ACROSS

3. Karen kept a _____ _____ (two words).
6. Mrs. _____ taught sixth grade.
8. The Newman house had a lot of _____.
12. Jeff's girlfriend, Mary Louise, smelled like _____.
13. Amy always got _____ after a long ride.
14. Jeff broke his _____ and walked with a cane.
15. Val read the entire *New York* _____ every Sunday.
16. Jeff vanished, or _____.
18. _____ was six years old.
23. Mrs. Newman hired a private _____ to find Jeff.
24. Spanish _____ (kind of food).
26. Val and Karen took a _____ bath.
27. Karen made a Viking _____ at school.
28. _____ Hall was where Mrs. Newman went to school.
29. The cat's name.

DOWN

1. Sunday breakfast was always _____.
2. Mrs. Newman got a _____ as a receptionist.
4. Amy enjoyed asking _____.
5. Petey Mansfield assured Karen that Jeff wasn't _____.
7. Mr. Newman owned a _____ store.
9. Mew liked _____ cat food.
10. Debbie and Karen went ice _____.
11. Debbie made _____ faces.
17. Mr. Newman moved to an _____.
19. The children called their grandfather _____.
20. _____ Dan.
21. Karen's mom and dad got a _____.
22. Mr. Newman went to Las _____.
25. _____ Ruth.

Johnny Tremain

By Esther Forbes

SEEK-A-WORD

```
A  R  O  T  C  O  D  R  N  I  A  M  E  R  T
B  P  C  A  I  R  L  T  S  Y  T  I  D  U  Y
T  O  R  S  H  N  A  Y  E  A  C  L  S  R  E
I  N  E  I  A  C  O  L  O  T  N  I  O  J  A
S  L  V  Y  N  I  T  I  N  R  L  T  S  P  C
A  T  O  S  D  T  N  B  M  V  O  I  L  N  R
N  I  L  N  A  I  E  E  E  R  S  A  R  O  U
N  V  U  B  R  O  H  R  B  I  T  E  T  R  C
A  D  T  E  A  I  S  T  E  A  L  U  S  E  I
H  A  I  N  O  M  E  Y  V  N  E  D  N  U  B
I  E  O  V  I  B  H  L  E  F  B  I  O  C  L
B  L  N  T  R  A  C  C  I  D  E  N  T  I  E
J  O  H  N  N  Y  E  U  T  L  R  B  S  P  M
T  I  E  L  C  T  A  P  N  I  E  N  O  L  D
S  N  A  I  D  N  I  H  O  T  R  H  B  I  C
```

WORDS:

Accident	Liberty
Battle	Militia
Boston	Printer
Crucible	Rebel
Cup	Revolution
Doctor	Silversmith
Hand	Steal
Johnny	Tea
Indians	Tory
Isannah	Tremain

Johnny Tremain

By Esther Forbes

CROSSWORD

ACROSS

1. Mr. _____ was a master silversmith.
4. _____ Harbor was closed by the British.
5. Goblin tumbled Lieutenant Strange in the _____.
6. The Lyte family _____ was on the coach and the cups.
7. The Blackbird was a man who was _____ and feathered.
9. All over New England people cast _____ for their guns.
11. The boys dressed like _____ for the tea party.
13. The war was fought "so that a _____ can stand up."
14. Johnny was apprenticed to a _____.
17. Priscilla's nickname.
18. The Boston _____ met in the Lorne's attic.
20. Johnny summoned the Observers by secret _____.
22. Rab made spicy _____ at the secret meetings.
23. "_____ Doodle," a song.
24. Isannah, the youngest girl, was _____.
25. Mr. Quincy was Johnny's _____.
27. General Gage was head of the _____ troops.

DOWN

1. Johnny's middle name.
2. _____ was shot by the firing squad.
3. Dr. _____ was at the Battle of Lexington.
4. One of the tea ships.
8. _____ was responsible for Johnny's accident.
10. Isannah went to live with Miss _____.
12. The Minutemen _____ at Lexington.
13. A _____ chased Merchant Lyte back to the city.
15. Rab died fighting for _____.
16. Johnny's _____ was burned badly.
19. _____ was a printer's apprentice.
20. Two lanterns were hung in the _____ spire.
21. Paul _____ owned a silver shop.
26. "School's done, _____'_ begun."

The Lion, the Witch, and the Wardrobe

By C. S. Lewis

SEEK-A-WORD

```
S  T  A  T  U  E  S  B  N  W  A  R  E  A  S
E  J  M  P  A  Z  H  E  T  Y  P  N  L  U  T
A  U  L  E  T  C  I  V  A  A  L  E  S  A  O
L  K  R  O  S  S  E  F  O  R  P  A  S  P  N
O  A  E  L  A  O  L  R  T  U  N  B  U  A  E
S  T  M  O  K  E  D  M  U  N  D  N  N  S  T
B  W  E  P  D  Q  R  O  A  L  E  A  M  R  A
E  N  R  S  P  N  T  L  K  T  S  M  U  J  B
B  D  T  N  A  O  S  M  W  E  L  U  T  E  L
O  V  E  Z  N  A  S  U  N  R  O  H  R  S  E
R  T  N  R  E  I  P  T  H  M  E  S  M  D  T
D  H  O  A  U  N  A  D  O  R  C  V  I  L  R
R  N  R  M  J  R  E  T  E  P  S  T  A  S  W
A  U  H  E  U  A  P  H  M  T  H  I  A  E  T
W  I  T  C  H  N  S  A  L  U  C  Y  T  W  B
```

WORDS:

Aslan
Beaver
Edmund
Horn
Human
Lamppost
Lucy
Mr. Tumnus
Narnia
Peter

Professor
Shield
Statues
Stone Table
Susan
Tea
Throne
War
Wardrobe
Witch

The Lion, the Witch, and the Wardrobe

By C. S. Lewis

CROSSWORD

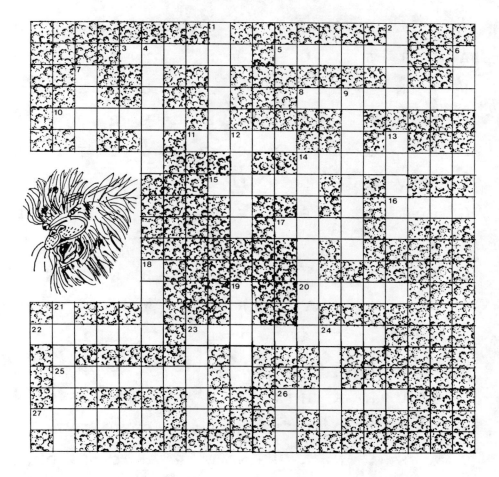

ACROSS

3. The _____ family took the children to meet Aslan.
5. The land of _____.
8. "You should never shut yourself up in a _____."
10. Mr. _____, the faun.
11. _____ freed the creatures who had been turned into statues.
14. Beings who are part horse, part man.
15. The White _____ called herself a queen.
16. Youngest of the children.
17. The _____ cut the cords which bound Aslan.
20. The Deep _____ had to be appeased.
22. City where the children lived.
23. The _____ lived in a famous old house.
25. Turkish _____.
26. When the witch's power was ended, _____ came.
27. There was a great _____ between the forces of the witch and those of Aslan.

DOWN

1. The grey wolf was named _____ Ulf.
2. The castle of _____ Paravel.
4. _____ was a traitor.
6. Daughter of _____.
7. Number of thrones in the castle.
9. _____ pulled the queen's sledge.
12. The others thought Lucy was _____ about her adventures.
13. The children met Aslan at the Stone _____.
14. Father _____.
18. Susan was given an ivory _____.
19. The witch turned her enemies into _____ statues.
21. Lucy received a bottle of _____.
23. _____ was to be High King.
24. Peter received a shield and _____.
26. _____ of Adam.

M.C. Higgins the Great

By Virginia Hamilton

SEEK-A-WORD

```
T  R  K  M  O  U  N  T  A  I  N  A  H  B  S
A  U  I  E  J  G  L  U  N  E  I  O  T  D  P
I  N  N  S  L  O  A  P  A  D  U  D  E  M  O
E  P  A  N  G  Q  N  C  E  B  E  P  Q  J  I
N  B  I  L  E  O  Y  E  G  M  W  S  T  E  L
R  N  V  E  K  L  N  L  S  N  I  G  G  I  H
U  E  K  U  N  E  U  F  E  K  T  O  E  S  E
B  A  T  I  D  N  P  N  I  P  C  I  C  F  A
L  E  K  N  A  I  I  E  N  E  H  N  O  N  P
L  S  A  R  N  V  L  R  D  N  Y  I  A  O  I
I  R  L  I  G  A  T  T  E  H  R  U  L  Y  L
K  N  I  F  E  R  I  V  O  G  A  E  N  I  A
L  T  U  N  R  H  G  A  U  I  N  L  E  S  N
N  R  C  T  O  E  W  H  E  O  R  I  P  M  K
B  A  N  I  N  A  J  N  L  P  U  O  S  D  C
```

WORDS:

Banina
Coal
Danger
Dude
Higgins
Jones
Killburn
Knife
Lake
Lurhetta

Mine
Mountain
Pole
Ravine
Singer
Soup
Spoil heap
Tunnel
Vine
Witchy

26

M.C. Higgins the Great

By Virginia Hamilton

CROSSWORD

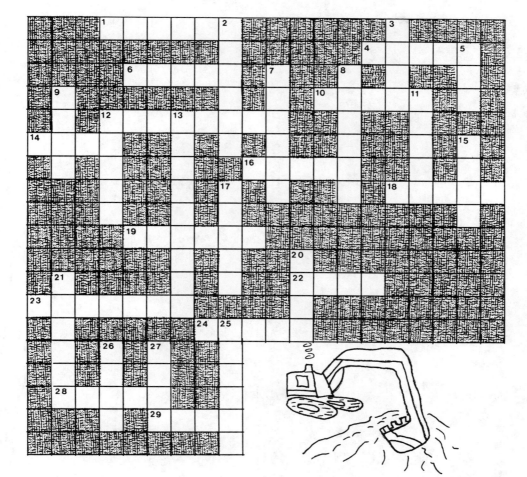

ACROSS

1. Jones made _____ soup.
4. M.C.'s father.
6. _____ potato pie.
10. Ben and M.C. used _____ to swing over the ravine.
12. Sarah's _____.
14. M.C.'s first name was _____.
16. Lurhetta left her _____ for M.C.
18. _____ heap.
19. Lurhetta _____ over by the lake.
22. _____ River.
23. The pole had a _____ seat on top.
24. Harenton was a _____ town.
28. The Higgins family would _____ as a signal.
29. The children went swimming in the _____.

DOWN

2. Lurhetta's last name.
3. M.C.'s prize.
5. Ben had _____ toes on each foot.
7. M.C.'s mother.
8. M.C. wanted his mother to become a famous _____.
9. M.C. caught a rabbit in his _____.
11. _____ mining.
12. Kill's _____.
13. M.C. had a _____ about the heap tumbling down.
15. Lurhetta couldn't _____.
17. M.C. Higgins the _____.
20. Black ore.
21. Folks said the Killburns were _____.
25. There was a water _____ between the lake and the pool.
26. The _____ carried a tape recorder.
27. M.C. started to build a _____ to protect the house.

Mrs. Frisby and the Rats of NIMH

By Robert C. O'Brien

SEEK-A-WORD

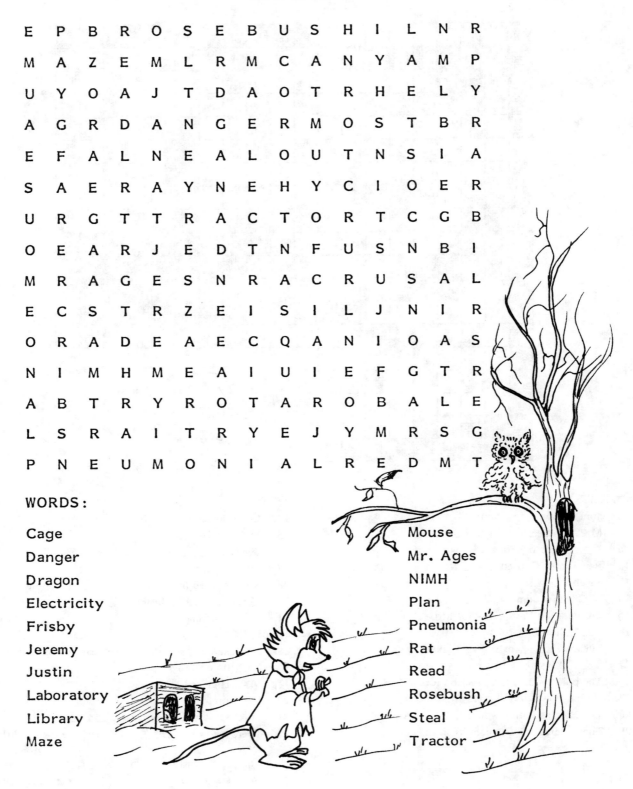

```
E  P  B  R  O  S  E  B  U  S  H  I  L  N  R
M  A  Z  E  M  L  R  M  C  A  N  Y  A  M  P
U  Y  O  A  J  T  D  A  O  T  R  H  E  L  Y
A  G  R  D  A  N  G  E  R  M  O  S  T  B  R
E  F  A  L  N  E  A  L  O  U  T  N  S  I  A
S  A  E  R  A  Y  N  E  H  Y  C  I  O  E  R
U  R  G  T  T  R  A  C  T  O  R  T  C  G  B
O  E  A  R  J  E  D  T  N  F  U  S  N  B  I
M  R  A  G  E  S  N  R  A  C  R  U  S  A  L
E  C  S  T  R  Z  E  I  S  I  L  J  N  I  R
O  R  A  D  E  A  E  C  Q  A  N  I  O  A  S
N  I  M  H  M  E  A  I  U  I  E  F  G  T  R
A  B  T  R  Y  R  O  T  A  R  O  B  A  L  E
L  S  R  A  I  T  R  Y  E  J  Y  M  R  S  G
P  N  E  U  M  O  N  I  A  L  R  E  D  M  T
```

WORDS:

Cage
Danger
Dragon
Electricity
Frisby
Jeremy
Justin
Laboratory
Library
Maze

Mouse
Mr. Ages
NIMH
Plan
Pneumonia
Rat
Read
Rosebush
Steal
Tractor

Mrs. Frisby and the Rats of NIMH

By Robert C. O'Brien

CROSSWORD

ACROSS

3. The men from _____ used nets to catch the mice.
5. Doctor _____.
8. Device used to test intelligence and memory.
9. The men used _____ gas.
12. The back tunnel came out in a _____ bramble.
14. Cat's name.
15. Side sheltered from the wind.
16. The rats lived under a _____.
21. The farm family was named _____.
22. _____ Valley.
23. The meeting was to discuss the _____.
25. Billy caught Mrs. Frisby in a _____.
27. The crow's name.
28. Mr. _____ gave Mrs. Frisby medicine for Timothy.
29. Used to pull a plow.

DOWN

1. The rats escaped through the air conditioner _____.
2. The rats had _____ lights.
4. The Frisbys were _____.
6. The owl lived in a _____ tree.
7. The Frisby family lived in a _____ block.
10. It's easy to unlock the door when you have the _____.
11. _____ Day.
13. The men took the rats to a _____.
17. Henderson's was a _____ store.
18. Mr. Ages mixed up a _____ powder for the cat.
19. _____ was the leader of the rats.
20. Timothy caught _____.
22. The Toy _____.
24. Leader of the rats who left the colony.
26. Jonathan Frisby had taught his wife and children to _____.

My Side of the Mountain

By Jean George

SEEK-A-WORD

```
E  M  N  R  G  S  M  O  C  C  A  S  I  N  S
M  T  E  I  E  R  N  E  W  R  T  F  R  H  U
O  O  L  Y  V  S  I  O  I  L  N  D  E  E  R
H  S  I  F  R  M  N  B  L  T  S  L  T  E  V
R  O  P  M  S  O  A  W  L  O  T  R  R  Q  I
W  V  D  O  T  U  S  A  F  E  U  S  O  L  V
E  S  O  M  C  N  K  I  R  A  Y  R  P  N  A
Z  H  O  C  A  T  S  K  I  L  L  S  E  E  L
V  R  W  O  S  A  G  R  S  I  H  C  R  P  K
Y  E  S  F  N  I  U  O  L  C  L  B  O  E  C
K  U  N  E  B  N  A  K  R  O  Y  W  E  N  O
L  D  O  I  A  A  L  M  O  W  E  A  H  R  L
S  N  O  W  S  T  O  R  M  C  Y  O  K  I  M
A  O  A  S  C  O  E  T  W  H  I  S  T  L  E
C  Y  B  A  R  O  N  A  R  U  M  H  N  R  H
```

WORDS:

Baron	New York
Catskills	Owls
Deer	Reporter
Falcon	Runaway
Fish	Shelter
Gribley	Snowstorm
Hemlock	Survival
Home	Venison
Moccasins	Whistle
Mountain	Woodpile

My Side of the Mountain

By Jean George

CROSSWORD

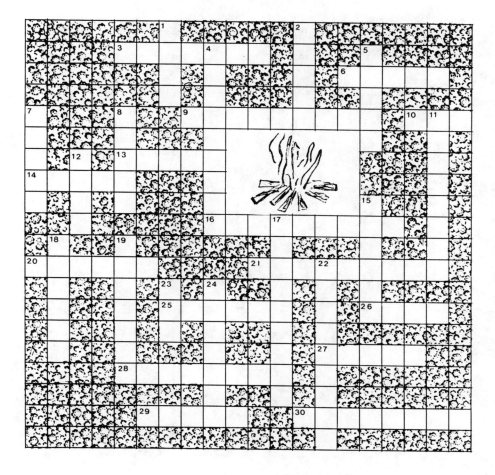

ACROSS

3. Sam's last name.
6. _____ was a college teacher.
9. The falcon's name.
10. A great horned _____.
13. _____ is rich in vitamin C.
14. Sam used _____ bark for paper.
16. Matt was a _____ reporter.
20. Tom's nickname was Mr. _____.
21. Indian shoes.
25. The fireplace was made of clay and _____.
26. Sam used a _____ to boil water in.
27. _____ and flint.
28. The smoke from the fire went out a _____.
29. _____ pancakes.
30. The _____ Mountains.

DOWN

1. _____ taught Sam how to build a fire.
2. Kind of fish.
4. Miss Turner was a _____.
5. _____ syrup.
7. Dogtooth violet _____ were good to eat.
8. The town Sam visited.
11. Willow _____ make good music.
12. _____ was one of Sam's favorite foods.
15. The Baron was a _____.
17. Used to walk on the snow.
18. Sam made underwear from _____ skins.
19. Sam's tree home was a _____ tree.
22. Sam had two visitors at _____.
23. The bed had _____ slats.
24. The _____ shot a deer out of season.

31

Old Yeller

By Fred Gipson

SEEK-A-WORD

```
C A B I N G W A T H G I F A T
T H F T A I H K F L N R Y S H
E O G N M O L U I J O E M K I
I T S I H R T O R H S I U O E
O F L O W P A Q L T D O G T F
U E L S G O H F W O R A F V S
X P I T N S L N X S I L R E H
S O H Y D R O P H O B I A O L
T L I E O V I G M I U D E G M
S C V L N T O O H S A H I L T
S A M L B R A Y I D I P O Q R
I T S E F I N K L H O V I S F
L E U R L X O A U R E L A W N
R O K A M E R H G P K T H R B
A C H U N T D F M I S A X E T
```

WORDS:

Arliss
Birdsong
Cabin
Dog
Farm
Fight
Hills
Hunt
Hurt
Hydrophobia

Knife
Love
Man
Plow
Shoot
Texas
Thief
Travis
Wolf
Yeller

Old Yeller

By Fred Gipson

CROSSWORD

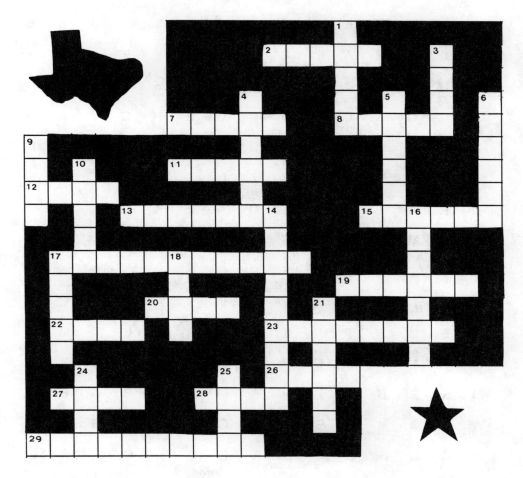

ACROSS

2. Travis had to _____ Yeller.
7. Log _____.
8. Black and white animal with a strong scent.
11. Where the story takes place.
12. Split _____ fence.
13. They carried Yeller on a _____.
15. Character telling the story.
17. Rabies.
19. Old _____.
20. The roan bull fell into a dump _____.
22. _____ lick.
23. _____ Creek.
26. Yeller's _____ had been bobbed.
27. Arliss tried to capture a _____ cub.
28. Travis got gashed in the leg by a hog's _____.
29. Travis's mother treated his leg with _____.

DOWN

1. The _____ tried to eat the corn and watermelons.
3. Travis taught Arliss how to throw a _____.
4. Arliss caught a _____ for his mother.
5. Mule's name.
6. Travis's last name.
9. Yellow vegetable with kernels.
10. A tall tale or big _____.
14. Bud Searcy's granddaughter.
16. The cattle drive ended in _____.
17. Mrs. Coates sewed Yeller's wound with _____ hair.
18. Prickly _____.
21. Little _____.
24. Travis went _____ hunting.
25. _____ Sanderson claimed Yeller was his dog.

33

Ramona and Her Father

By Beverly Cleary

SEEK-A-WORD

```
C O M M E R C I A L S Y S E B
L I Z R A L E S H R P E U O R
B H G M T R B V A T S R J E B
A U O A I S F K C E H C Y A P
C N R S R A E B Y M M U G R F
A I E S B E E Z U S I H L I E
P R A T M A T O A E A O R C S
L E M I H E S T Y S C W V H A
A T S L O G F R E H M I E W M
Y A I T E A V U I S A E O C T
L E M S T N E S E R P L Q M S
I J K H C O R P H A E N A Y I
M S E B M I H A M B U R G E R
A R O Y P S T U C G M T B O H
F C U S G E B S R E L O R A C
```

WORDS:

Beezus

Burs

Carolers

Christmas

Cigarettes

Commercial

Family

Father

Gummy bears

Hamburger

Howie

Job

Noise

Paycheck

Pest

Play

Presents

Ramona

Sheep

Stilts

Ramona and Her Father

By Beverly Cleary

CROSSWORD

ACROSS

3. Henry _____.
5. _____ was Ramona's sister.
8. Ramona's _____ friend was Howie.
9. Ramona eavesdropped on her parents through the _____ pipes.
10. Ramona wanted a _____ costume.
11. _____ burger.
15. "_____ is hazardous to your health."
17. Beezus was _____ in the Christmas pageant.
19. Ramona's father got a job as a supermarket _____.
20. Tin _____ stilts.
22. Ramona's father lost his _____.
23. _____ River.
27. "First time is funny, second time is _____."
28. Ramona was in _____ grade.
29. _____-toes (tomatoes).
30. Chewy bear-shaped candy.

DOWN

1. A crown of _____.
2. Mrs. Swink used to call some of the other children "_____."
4. Spoiled _____.
6. Mr. Quimby had to stand in an _____ line.
7. Ramona made out her Christmas list in _____.
12. A jack-o'-lantern is carved from a _____.
13. Ramona wanted to earn money making TV _____.
14. Picky _____, the cat.
16. _____ School.
18. The three wise _____.
21. Ramona's last name.
24. _____ meant treats.
25. Coocoo (cuckoo) _____.
26. Mrs. Quimby worked for a _____.

The Slave Dancer

By Paula Fox

SEEK-A-WORD

```
S  L  A  V  E  P  R  A  E  L  K  F  N  B  E
W  H  R  N  I  D  E  C  A  N  D  L  E  S  V
A  V  I  W  A  N  O  I  Q  E  I  A  W  A  I
E  S  O  P  R  E  A  R  A  C  M  P  O  E  T
I  P  D  Y  W  S  L  F  I  G  O  S  R  Y  P
T  N  I  B  A  R  R  A  C  O  O  N  L  I  A
O  R  T  S  P  G  E  N  D  E  N  P  E  W  C
E  H  A  C  P  A  E  C  R  A  L  F  A  T  V
S  I  E  D  R  V  I  O  K  L  I  O  N  C  Y
L  F  C  A  E  A  S  L  E  F  G  E  S  A  R
E  S  P  I  N  L  S  D  R  N  H  Y  L  H  S
I  L  E  D  T  A  E  O  I  O  T  P  R  D  A
N  G  M  A  I  R  J  A  M  C  E  K  O  E  M
A  T  E  N  C  O  K  E  N  S  H  L  J  S  V
D  A  N  C  E  R  D  E  P  P  A  N  D  I  K
```

WORDS: U.S.A.

Africa
Apprentice
Barracoon
Candles
Captive
Dancer
Daniel
Fife
Home
Jessie

AFRICA

Kidnapped
Moonlight
New Orleans
Play
Ras
Sail
Shipwreck
Slave
Trade
Voyage

The Slave Dancer

By Paula Fox

CROSSWORD

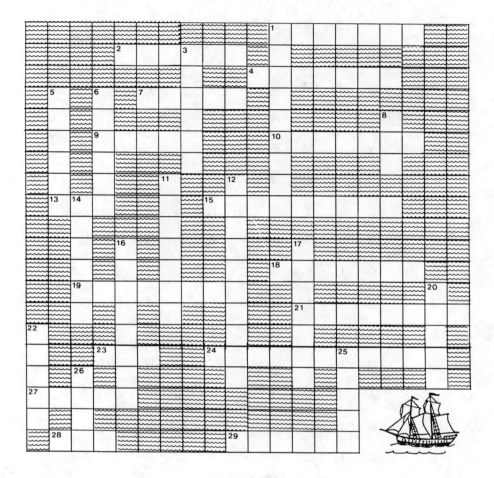

ACROSS

1. The War _____ the States.
2. Cat's _____, a game played with a piece of string.
4. New _____, a city in Louisiana.
7. Jessie's job was to _____ the slaves.
9. _____ Island, a state.
10. Type of sailing ship.
13. The black boy.
15. Ship Jessie sailed on.
18. On shipboard Jessie slept in a _____.
19. _____ of lime.
21. Jessie's age.
23. Alcoholic drink.
24. _____ River.
27. Cat-o'-nine _____, a type of whip.
28. _____ was the ship's carpenter.
29. _____ dreamed of becoming rich.

DOWN

1. Slaves were held in a _____.
3. _____ was an escaped slave.
5. Cawthorne was known as a tight _____.
6. _____ was one of the men who captured Jessie.
8. A beverage which can be hot or cold.
11. Religious group which opposed slavery.
12. Jessie's nickname.
14. One of the seven continents.
16. Sailing ships were often becalmed in the _____.
17. _____ Cawthorne.
20. The Bight of _____.
22. Jessie's sister.
25. The _____ trade was called "black gold."
26. Instrument Jessie played.

The Summer of the Swans

By Betsy Byars

SEEK-A-WORD

```
P  E  D  L  P  S  R  E  M  M  U  S  A  R  A
O  A  I  U  L  W  L  T  A  L  A  N  E  T  S
L  O  R  E  T  A  R  D  E  D  I  E  R  C  E
I  E  Q  T  B  U  K  R  S  H  M  A  F  P  L
C  P  A  E  Y  N  M  E  W  R  V  K  T  W  O
E  S  R  N  S  T  N  O  A  I  A  E  A  R  S
O  A  I  U  C  W  Y  R  N  H  C  R  N  E  T
E  M  P  K  A  I  A  E  S  A  E  S  A  M  P
S  A  E  N  O  L  S  T  E  I  K  C  T  J  L
L  J  D  T  E  L  I  H  C  R  A  E  S  O  R
R  A  R  L  A  I  D  S  A  H  O  M  E  A  E
D  P  E  N  H  E  L  N  Q  E  V  W  R  H  O
E  C  U  S  J  A  C  O  K  S  A  U  O  A  J
S  A  D  C  R  O  W  A  T  J  M  P  F  S  R
W  P  T  F  E  I  L  R  A  H  C  A  E  A  W
```

WORDS:

Aunt Willie

Charlie

Forest

Home

Joe

Lake

Lost

Pajamas

Party

Police

Puce

Ravine

Retarded

Sara

Search

Sneakers

Summer

Swans

Wanda

Watch

The Summer of the Swans

By Betsy Byars

CROSSWORD

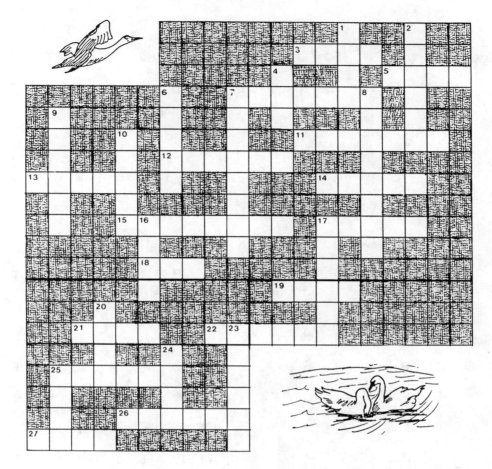

ACROSS

3. Mr. Godfrey worked in _____.
5. Aunt Willie thought Charlie was in an old _____.
7. Aunt Willie rode Frank's motor _____.
11. _____ was important to Charlie.
12. _____ kool-aid.
13. Sara's sister.
14. Joe invited Sara to a _____.
15. Bedroom _____. (Hint: worn on feet.)
17. Sara and Charlie fed the swans some _____.
18. Number of swans on the lake.
19. _____ Virginia (state).
21. Charlie couldn't _____.
22. Original color of Sara's sneakers.
25. Aunt Willie called the _____ when Charlie was missing.
26. There was a _____ missing from Charlie's pajamas.
27. Sara's _____ friend was Mary.

DOWN

1. A barbed _____ fence.
2. "Property of State _____."
4. Sara thought _____ had stolen Charlie's watch.
6. Charlie was proud of his _____.
7. Everybody _____ for Charlie.
8. Charlie was _____.
9. _____ duck.
10. Sara took Charlie to see the _____.
16. Charlie got _____ in the woods.
17. Sara's dog.
20. Charlie kicked his foot against the _____.
23. A deep cut in the earth.
24. Sara fixed a _____ for Charlie.
25. Sara dyed her sneakers _____.

Tuck Everlasting

By Natalie Babbitt

SEEK-A-WORD

```
W  G  M  K  U  P  A  G  E  E  R  T  M  S  R
L  I  R  I  S  E  L  O  I  H  V  N  F  O  E
S  H  N  B  G  K  M  E  W  D  O  O  W  K  T
A  T  S  N  L  D  A  P  V  I  T  B  E  L  A
R  I  F  J  I  U  N  U  G  T  O  H  S  C  W
E  O  D  P  N  E  O  E  N  A  V  A  P  V  T
V  A  C  E  T  A  S  I  T  R  O  N  R  A  G
E  S  R  O  H  C  F  K  B  M  U  S  I  C  L
R  U  D  N  G  Q  I  J  C  H  R  A  N  P  T
O  A  R  S  I  D  L  O  I  A  E  U  G  O  E
F  E  M  J  N  P  A  E  S  G  J  A  I  L  I
D  K  R  A  D  F  O  H  R  G  K  P  V  F  T
A  D  P  O  I  C  T  S  B  A  I  E  A  M  S
O  W  I  A  M  A  G  I  C  O  S  U  R  L  W
T  U  C  K  W  P  O  F  W  H  N  I  N  T  F
```

WORDS:

Elves
Fish
Flapjacks
Forever
Horse
Jail
Kidnap
Magic
Man
Midnight

Music
Rowboat
Shotgun
Spring
Toad
Treegap
Tuck
Water
Winnie
Wood

Tuck Everlasting
By Natalie Babbitt

CROSSWORD

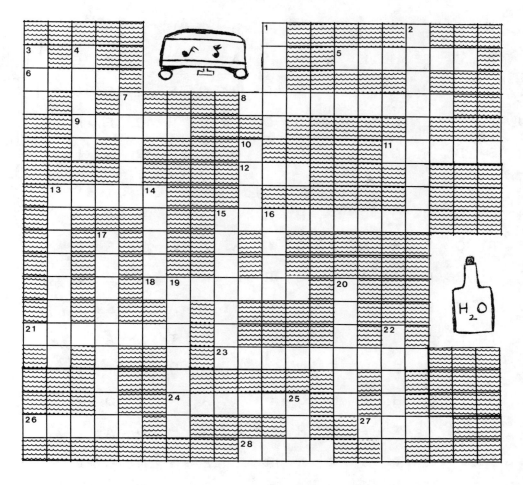

ACROSS

5. The water from the _____ was magic.
6. Winnie's house had an _____ fence around it.
8. The Tuck family _____ Winnie.
9. "_____ walls do not a prison make."
11. Granny said the _____ made the music.
12. There was a giant _____ tree at the center of the wood.
13. _____ and Winnie went fishing.
15. Pancakes.
18. Village where story takes place.
21. Mae hit the stranger with a _____.
23. Jesse was _____ years old.
24. Hot summer month.
26. Tuck compared life to a _____.
27. Winnie poured the magic water on the _____.
28. The Tuck's house was beside a _____.

DOWN

1. Mae had a little _____ box.
2. Lightning bugs.
3. The Tuck family could never _____.
4. A _____ lived in the table drawer.
7. The stranger stole Tuck's _____.
10. Jesse and Miles helped Mae to escape from _____.
13. 12:00 A.M.
14. Jesse and Miles _____ in the loft.
15. Winnie said the Tucks were her _____.
16. Miles's daughter's name.
17. The _____ arrested Mae.
19. Winnie decided to _____ _____ (two words).
20. Winnie _____.
22. The stranger wore a _____ suit.
25. Mae and Tuck saw their boys every _____ years.

Twenty and Ten

By Claire H. Bishop

SEEK-A-WORD

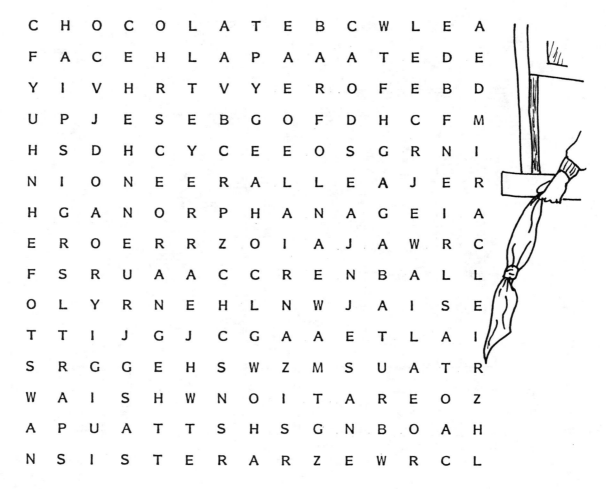

```
C  H  O  C  O  L  A  T  E  B  C  W  L  E  A
F  A  C  E  H  L  A  P  A  A  A  T  E  D  E
Y  I  V  H  R  T  V  Y  E  R  O  F  E  B  D
U  P  J  E  S  E  B  G  O  F  D  H  C  F  M
H  S  D  H  C  Y  C  E  E  O  S  G  R  N  I
N  I  O  N  E  E  R  A  L  L  E  A  J  E  R
H  G  A  N  O  R  P  H  A  N  A  G  E  I  A
E  R  O  E  R  R  Z  O  I  A  J  A  W  R  C
F  S  R  U  A  A  C  C  R  E  N  B  A  L  L
O  L  Y  R  N  E  H  L  N  W  J  A  I  S  E
T  T  I  J  G  J  C  G  A  A  E  T  L  A  I
S  R  G  G  E  H  S  W  Z  M  S  U  A  T  R
W  A  I  S  H  W  N  O  I  T  A  R  E  O  Z
A  P  U  A  T  T  S  H  S  G  N  B  O  A  H
N  S  I  S  T  E  R  A  R  Z  E  W  R  C  L
```

WORDS:

Ball
Before
Cave
Chocolate
Coalshed
Egypt
Flight
France
Henry
Hide

Jesus
Jews
Miracle
Nazis
Orange
Orphanage
Ration
Rutabaga
Sister
War

42

Twenty and Ten
By Claire H. Bishop

CROSSWORD

ACROSS

1. The Nazis hated _____.
3. _____ and potato soup was Henry's favorite.
5. Louis said his name was _____.
7. Jesus' family were fleeing from _____ soldiers.
9. Number of Jewish children brought to the orphanage.
11. Arthur gave Henry some _____.
13. Beauvallon was an old house on top of a _____.
14. The _____ into Egypt.
19. Louis thought the _____ were balls.
20. The girls fixed _____ for lunch.
22. _____ was jealous of Janet.
23. The _____ were German.
24. The soldiers called the children nasty _____.
26. Henry hid his "treasures" under a _____.

DOWN

2. A _____ handkerchief was the all-clear signal.
3. Denise's little brother.
4. The Jewish children hid in a _____.
6. _____ cards.
8. _____ was the village near the orphanage.
9. Number of children in the orphanage.
10. Country where the story takes place.
11. The Nazis locked Henry in the _____.
12. The multiplication of loaves and _____.
15. Sister _____.
16. The children all became _____.
17. The children had a _____ of bread and apples.
18. Character who tells the story.
21. The older Nazi smoked a _____.
25. "We _____ eat or no one eats."

43

The Upstairs Room

By Johanna Reiss

SEEK-A-WORD

```
B F S S R I A T S P U R E N E
C I O O I A H O J D R A S I L
O R C L O S E T N X T S N C A
H O N Y W Z U A O F I N Y S A
R A W O C A L P R U A A C I L
I M O I K L E R B P D R C B E
E C L W O E E I H L K C M O O
O N A H O J T S H Z C K O Z C
B A S R B H A N W M U O R K N
U Z A S N N O I S E R A C N Y
H I D E D A I T I L T R I W C
T S E W A O D N L S C H O O L
R W R I S O A N O I N R D O N
P O P O E I R I S N K I R E M
J C E E B S T O A I A O N K O
```

WORDS:

Annie
Bicycle
Book
Closet
Cows
Farm
Hide
Holland
Johan
Nazis

Noise
Opoe
Radio
Room
School
Sini
Star
Truck
Upstairs
War

The Upstairs Room
By Johanna Reiss

CROSSWORD

ACROSS

1. Dientje borrowed _____ from the minister.
7. Mr. DeLeeuw wanted to go to _____.
9. The _____ Army liberated Ussilo.
11. Granny _____.
12. Name given to the soldiers who fought the Germans.
14. Johan worked in the _____.
15. Annie did not like hiding in the _____.
17. _____ were illegal.
18. Annie went downstairs to get some _____.
19. Notices were posted on a _____.
23. Annie's sister.
25. Annie needed to _____ her muscles.
27. This story takes place in _____.
28. Second World _____.
29. Johan got _____ identification papers for Sini.

DOWN

1. Annie's dog.
2. _____ Oosterveld.
3. The Oostervelds were _____.
4. Hitler hated the _____.
5. The first family Annie stayed with.
6. Dini gave Annie a _____ game.
8. The Nazis took part of the Oosterveld's _____ for their headquarters.
10. The girls had a hiding place in the _____.
13. Food was _____.
16. The main character in this story.
20. Sini dyed her hair _____.
21. Rachel cut Annie's _____.
22. Miss Kleinhoonte was a _____.
24. Jews had to wear a _____ star.
26. _____ was Annie's oldest sister.

The Westing Game

By Ellin Raskin

SEEK-A-WORD

```
G A M E N V E L O P E T A T M
N I L L E S M K E E R C W I L
I S E G D U J O R C W A S E S
T V T W H M A I F A T T I G R
S B T I R E H N I U A R T I E
E J T U E L F P R K R E S T N
W I B N H E R T E O Z E O E T
E I S H A L L O W E E N P S R
E O L M G E E L O N N O E A A
U E R L U N L U R O Y T R A P
W S I E C R R H K S H E K N S
L R E O P D D P S S R B E R P
W I D U M U E E E A R O O U S
P E K A L M H O R T E O I M T
O H P R G C R O W N R K Y R B
```

WORDS:

Bomb
Chess
Clues
Crow
Envelope
Fireworks
Game
Halloween
Heirs
Inherit

Judge
Mistake
Murder
Notebook
Paper
Partners
Party
Turtle
Westing
Will

46

The Westing Game

By Ellin Raskin

CROSSWORD

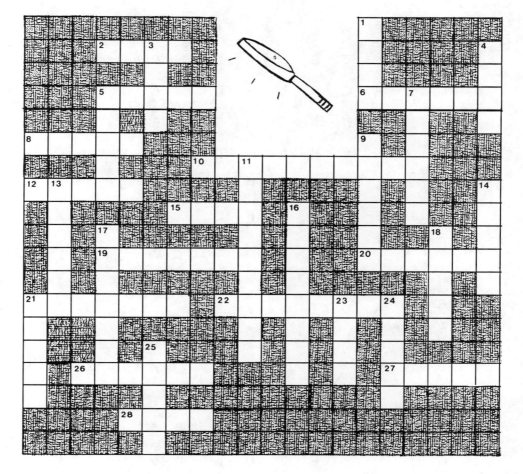

ACROSS

2. Sunset Towers faced _____.
5. Mrs. Hoo wanted to go back to _____.
6. Angela wanted to be a _____.
8. "Buy Westing _____ Products!"
10. Sandy _____.
12. Hoo's On _____.
15. Last _____ and testament.
19. "_____ the Beautiful."
20. _____ Wexler.
21. Sam _____.
22. Lake _____.
26. _____ set off the fireworks.
27. Number of teams trying to solve the mystery.
28. _____ married Otis Amber.

DOWN

1. J.J. _____ was a judge.
3. Where Turtle kicked people.
4. Chris was a _____ watcher.
5. Theo and Mr. Westing both played _____.
7. "It's what you don't have that _____."
9. Otis wore a leather aviator's _____.
11. Good _____ Soup Kitchen.
13. Mr. Hoo invented a paper _____.
14. Hints to a mystery.
16. Barney _____.
17. Julian R. _____.
18. Turtle played the _____ market.
21. Turtle's Halloween costume.
23. Doug won a _____ medal.
24. Sydelle Pulaski took shorthand _____ at the reading of the will.
25. "_____, beware."

Where the Lilies Bloom

By Bill Cleaver and Vera Cleaver

SEEK-A-WORD

```
D  N  C  M  A  R  Y  C  A  L  L  R  A  O  G
O  E  M  Y  T  E  N  A  O  A  C  N  R  I  I
M  D  V  A  G  S  L  E  W  A  G  O  N  O  D
O  A  L  O  N  I  O  N  S  O  C  S  E  L  I
U  E  V  N  L  K  E  G  I  T  E  V  A  C  D
N  S  W  L  R  A  Y  E  R  N  R  S  N  W  M
T  A  H  S  N  E  D  F  G  Y  O  R  A  A  R
A  L  W  I  L  D  C  R  A  F  T  E  R  N  S
I  H  I  L  O  S  I  M  A  R  L  R  Z  T  G
N  D  A  R  O  T  V  Y  S  Z  Y  I  M  O  A
L  V  T  R  E  E  R  G  A  G  Z  E  V  O  A
D  R  O  U  Z  N  U  A  S  R  L  I  A  R  T
R  O  I  D  A  R  L  U  A  I  I  O  L  T  D
D  T  A  U  D  O  E  Y  R  L  R  A  E  B  K
I  G  B  R  E  H  T  U  L  Y  O  R  N  I  B
```

WORDS:

Bear
Blizzard
Cave
Devola
Dig
Drugs
Ginseng
Hornets
Kiser
Marry

Mary Call
Mountain
Onions
Radio
Root
Roy Luther
Trail
Valley
Wagon
Wildcrafter

48

Where the Lilies Bloom

By Bill Cleaver and Vera Cleaver

CROSSWORD

ACROSS

3. Mary Call's age.
5. Goldie was Kiser's _____.
9. Mary Call made a poultice of _____ for Kiser.
10. Person who picks wild medicine plants.
13. _____ was "cloudy-headed."
14. A witch's _____ in the chimney.
16. Romey was the only _____ in the Luther family.
19. Mary Call did not want to accept _____.
20. Season after winter.
22. Kiser _____ wanted to marry Devola.
24. The _____ of the school, Miss Breathitt.
26. A black bird.
28. The narrator of this story (two words).
29. _____ Smoky Mountains.

DOWN

1. Breed of red and white cows.
2. Old _____, a mountain.
4. The Luthers were _____ farmers.
6. Ima Dean cut paper dolls from a _____ catalog.
7. Romey made Christmas _____.
8. Kiser bought Devola a _____.
11. _____ _____ died (two words).
12. Poor no-account mountaineer, a happy _____.
15. Romey chased Mrs. Connell with a stuffed _____.
16. Fierce snowstorm.
17. Witch _____ (medicinal plant).
18. Kiser signed over twenty _____ of land to the Luthers.
21. Mr. Connell ran the _____ store.
23. _____ was bringing $30.00 per pound.
25. _____ Valley.
27. The Luthers ate fried corn _____ mush.

The Witch of Blackbird Pond

By Elizabeth G. Speare

SEEK-A-WORD

```
B  S  W  I  T  C  H  A  N  N  A  H  D  N  V
A  C  N  G  H  L  C  K  O  O  B  N  R  O  H
R  A  W  D  A  E  R  A  I  U  R  I  Y  C  N
B  E  C  N  E  D  U  R  P  N  C  A  T  E  D
A  O  A  O  I  T  H  K  N  R  G  E  P  N  T
D  I  T  H  N  O  C  E  D  E  S  N  U  A  N
O  C  G  R  A  N  D  F  A  T  H  E  R  T  H
S  I  U  T  G  I  E  D  O  L  P  H  I  N  E
G  C  A  L  D  M  H  C  R  L  K  I  T  O  S
A  N  H  R  C  R  A  W  T  A  P  O  A  R  W
R  E  I  N  E  I  N  E  A  I  A  K  N  A  O
M  H  F  K  M  T  O  Y  N  R  C  H  U  H  D
P  T  A  E  S  D  S  U  R  T  O  U  T  B  A
V  U  O  R  A  U  K  R  A  U  I  N  T  Q  E
Q  E  G  E  M  O  H  W  O  K  H  S  W  I  M
```

WORDS:

Barbados
Church
Connecticut
Dolphin
Grandfather
Hannah
Home
Hornbook
Husking
Kit

Meadows
Nat
Prudence
Puritan
Quaker
Read
Swim
Trial
Voyage
Witch

The Witch of Blackbird Pond

By Elizabeth G. Speare

CROSSWORD

ACROSS

3. Dr. Bulkeley had a _____ tooth.
4. The beginners in school used a _____.
5. _____, Connecticut was Kit's new home in America.
7. Kit dragged Hannah through the woods to avoid the _____.
10. Dr. Gershom Bulkeley was minister at the _____ house.
12. The young folks attended a husking _____.
13. _____ was first mate and the captain's son.
14. Kit jumped in the Connecticut _____ to retrieve the doll.
16. Hannah's magic cure was blueberry _____ and a kitten.
18. William Ashby came _____ Kit.
19. Hannah Tupper was known as a _____.
20. John Holbrook joined the _____.
21. Kit Tyler came from _____.
24. The townfolks burned Hannah's _____.
25. Kit was used to having _____ wait on her.
28. The wool was washed, bleached, and _____.
29. The one ornament in Hannah's house was a piece of _____.
30. Kit had never seen _____ before.

DOWN

1. Judith and Mercy came down with the _____.
2. _____ Cruff hated Kit.
6. Kit was considered a _____ by her uncle.
8. What the children wrote on, curly birch _____.
9. _____ and Judith were Kit's cousins.
11. Kit went to the _____ Meadow for comfort.
15. The Woods family were _____ (their religion).
17. The charter was stolen on _____ Hallows' Eve.
22. The name of the ship Kit sailed to America on.
23. Kit was put in a _____ with only straw in it.
26. Matthew Wood was a very _____ man.
27. Blackbird Pond was Kit's favorite _____.

51

ANSWERS

The Best Christmas Pageant Ever

By Barbara Robinson

SEEK-A-WORD

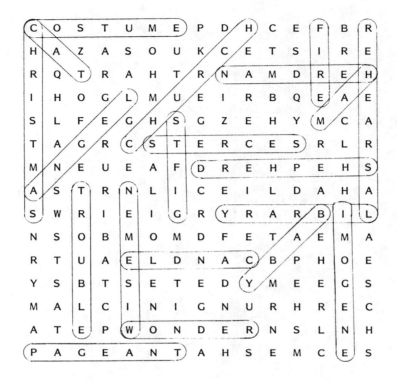

CROSSWORD

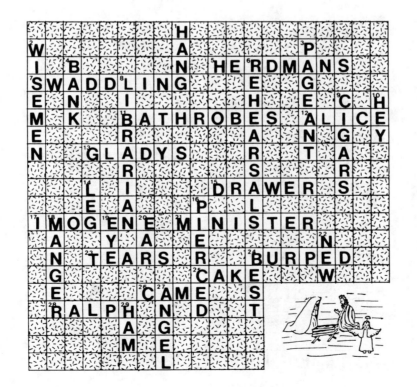

The Black Pearl
By Scott O'Dell

SEEK-A-WORD

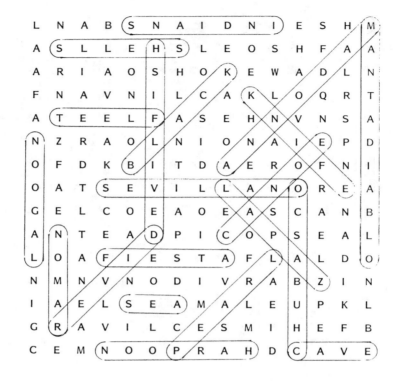

CROSSWORD

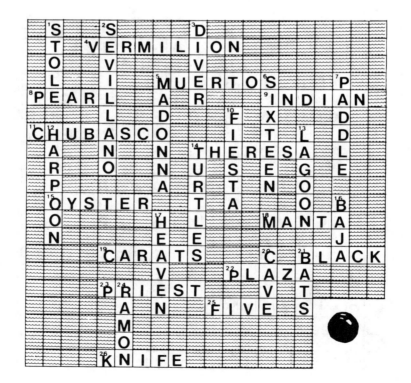

The Borrowers
By Mary Norton

SEEK-A-WORD

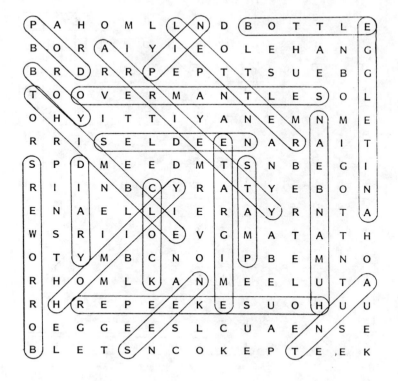

CROSSWORD

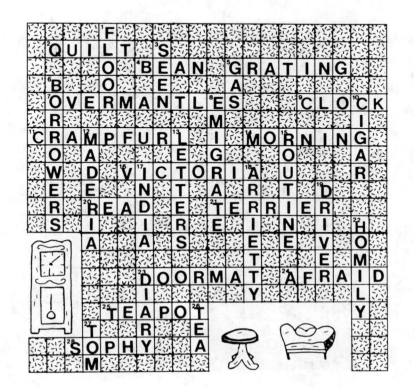

The Cabin Faced West
By Jean Fritz

SEEK-A-WORD

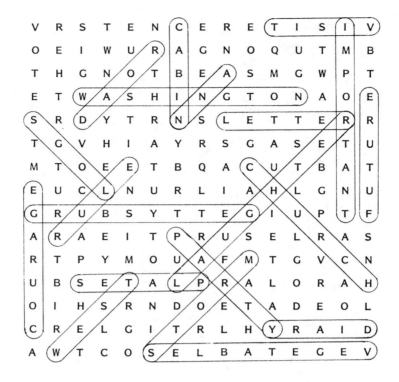

CROSSWORD

Chitty Chitty Bang Bang

By Ian Fleming

SEEK-A-WORD

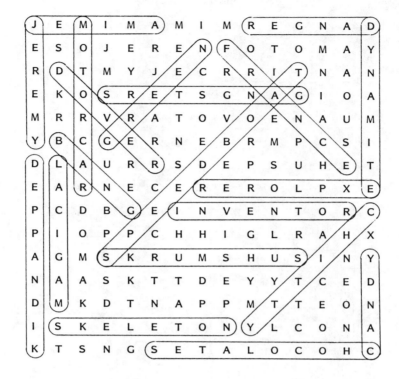

```
J  E  M  I  M  A  M  I  M  R  E  G  N  A  D
E  S  O  J  E  R  E  N  F  O  T  O  M  A  Y
R  D  T  M  Y  J  E  C  R  R  I  T  N  A  N
E  K  O  S  R  E  T  S  G  N  A  G  I  O  A
M  R  R  V  R  A  T  O  V  O  E  N  A  U  M
Y  B  C  G  E  R  N  E  B  R  M  P  C  S  I
D  L  A  U  R  R  S  D  E  P  S  U  H  E  T
E  C  D  B  G  E  I  N  V  E  N  T  O  R  C
P  I  O  P  P  C  H  H  I  G  L  R  A  H  X
P  G  M  S  K  R  U  M  S  H  U  S  I  N  Y
A  A  A  S  K  T  T  D  E  Y  Y  T  C  E  D
N  M  K  D  T  N  A  P  P  M  T  T  E  O  N
D  I  S  K  E  L  E  T  O  N  Y  L  C  O  N  A
K  T  S  N  G  S  E  T  A  L  O  C  O  H  C
```

CROSSWORD

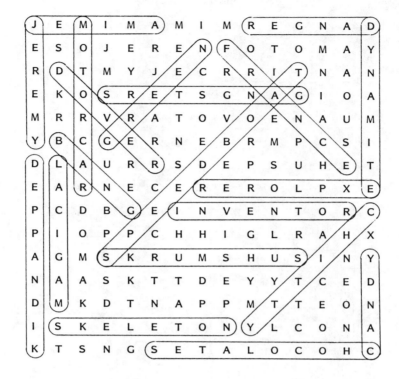

59

The Door in the Wall
By Marguerite De Angeli

SEEK-A-WORD

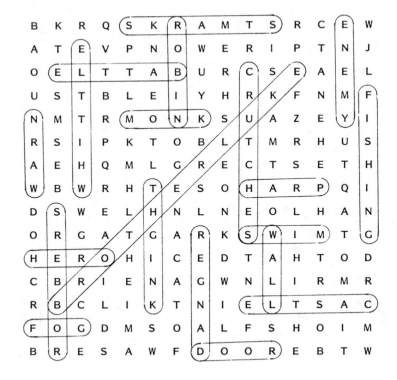

CROSSWORD

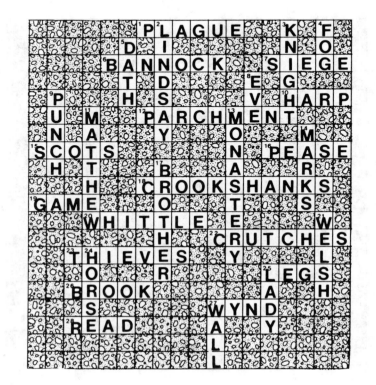

The Great Gilly Hopkins

By Katherine Paterson

SEEK-A-WORD

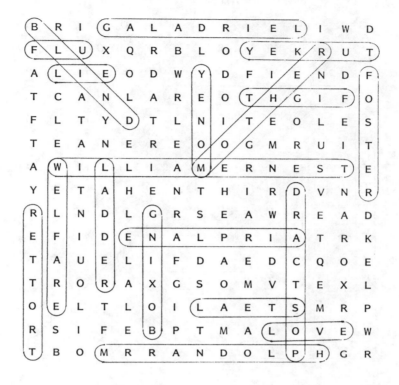

CROSSWORD

61

Harriet the Spy

By Louise Fitzhugh

SEEK-A-WORD

CROSSWORD

The Incredible Journey

By Sheila Burnford

SEEK-A-WORD

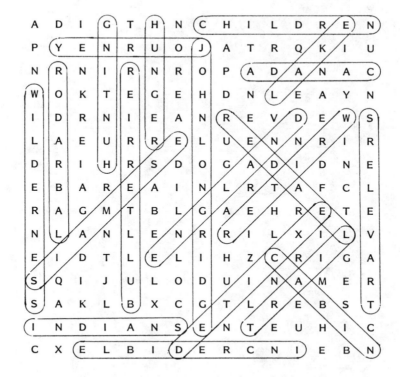

CROSSWORD

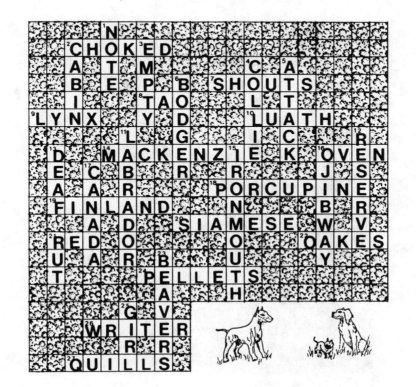

It's Not the End of the World

By Judy Blume

SEEK-A-WORD

```
O  G  J  F  E  T  D  R  S  V  D  L  R  O  W
E  I  P  L  I  O  N  I  C  R  E  A  N  M  E
A  E  Y  K  A  R  E  N  H  W  T  W  A  I  D
G  R  B  O  S  L  Y  H  O  Q  D  Y  L  J  W
D  I  V  O  R  C  E  R  O  M  C  E  K  I  F
E  J  O  B  E  S  M  E  L  B  O  R  P  M  F
S  K  E  Y  L  O  A  C  I  R  L  H  A  T  E
S  W  D  A  P  A  R  T  M  E  N  T  K  L  J
E  T  W  D  O  B  R  E  F  C  O  U  E  O  F
R  D  S  N  V  E  I  R  L  N  S  R  A  P  Q
T  E  H  T  F  O  A  T  K  R  F  I  G  H  T
D  V  I  K  I  N  G  S  A  G  B  O  N  C  L
A  O  A  B  J  O  E  D  Q  R  E  K  Y  D  U
E  M  E  W  F  A  L  M  O  V  W  M  P  S  A
W  S  L  K  H  S  N  I  S  D  N  E  I  R  F
```

CROSSWORD

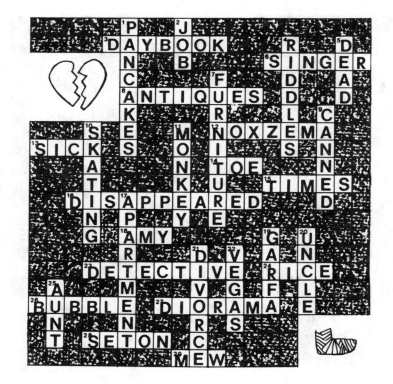

Johnny Tremain

By Esther Forbes

SEEK-A-WORD

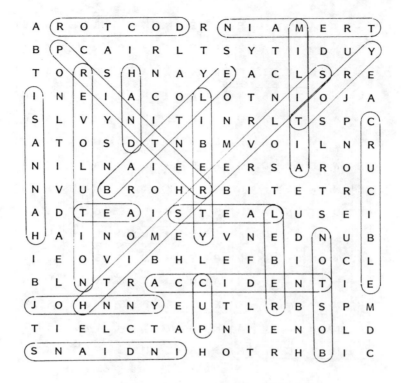

CROSSWORD

The Lion, the Witch, and the Wardrobe

By C. S. Lewis

SEEK-A-WORD

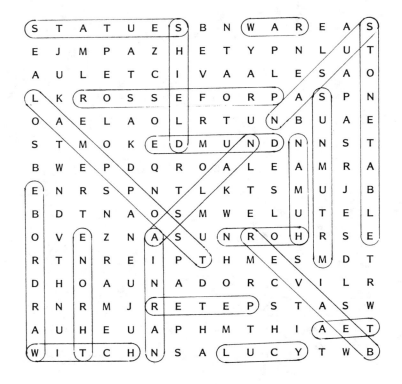

CROSSWORD

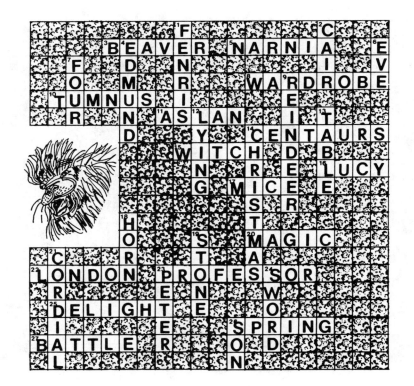

M.C. Higgins the Great

By Virginia Hamilton

SEEK-A-WORD

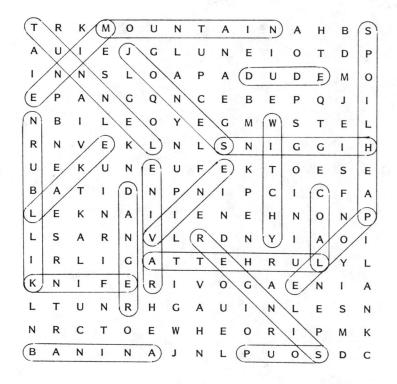

CROSSWORD

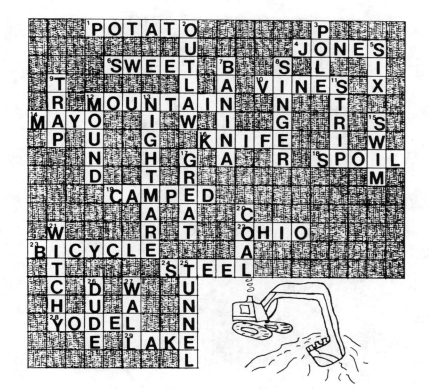

Mrs. Frisby and the Rats of NIMH

By Robert C. O'Brien

SEEK-A-WORD

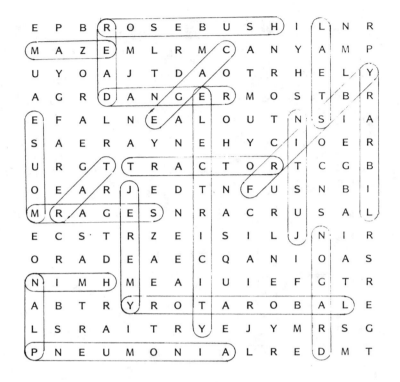

CROSSWORD

My Side of the Mountain

By Jean George

SEEK-A-WORD

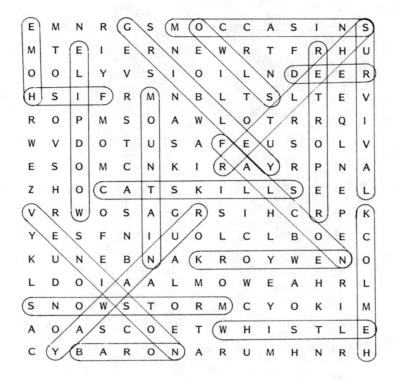

CROSSWORD

Old Yeller
By Fred Gipson

SEEK-A-WORD

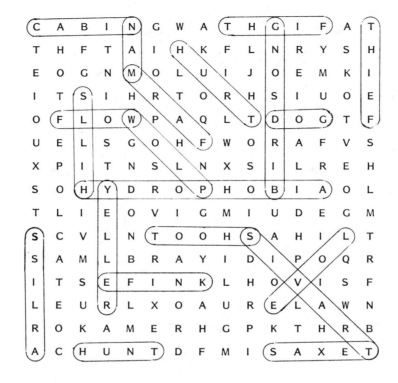

CROSSWORD

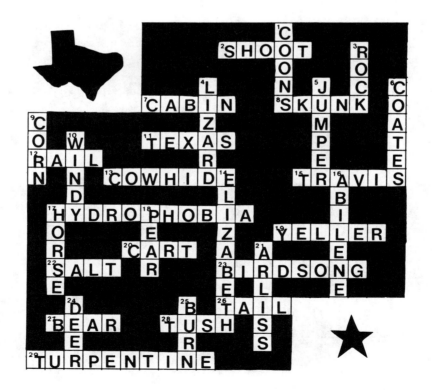

Ramona and Her Father

By Beverly Cleary

SEEK-A-WORD

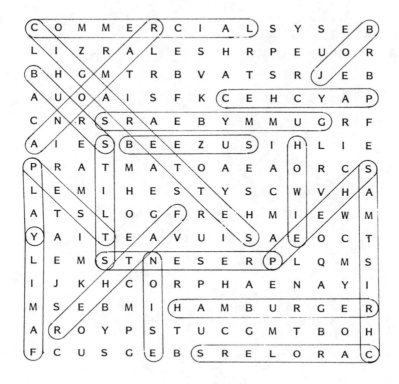

CROSSWORD

The Slave Dancer
By Paula Fox

SEEK-A-WORD

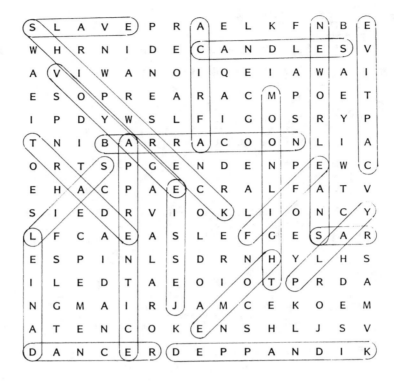

CROSSWORD

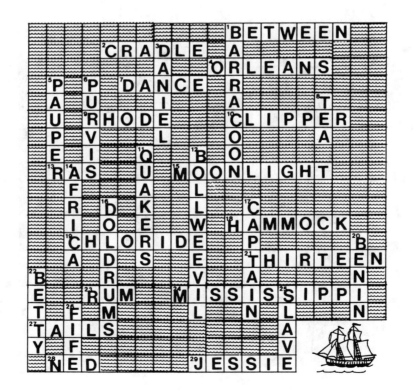

The Summer of the Swans

By Betsy Byars

SEEK-A-WORD

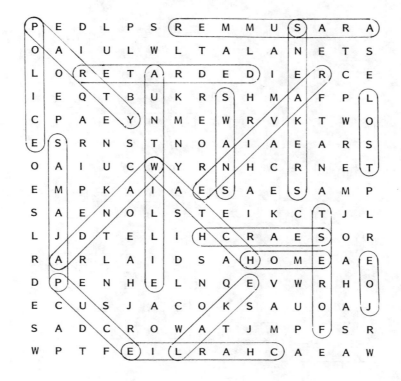

CROSSWORD

Tuck Everlasting
By Natalie Babbitt

SEEK-A-WORD

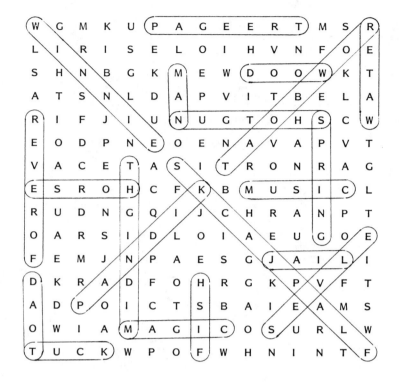

CROSSWORD

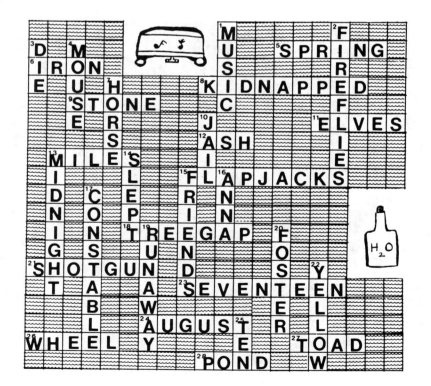

Twenty and Ten

By Claire H. Bishop

SEEK-A-WORD

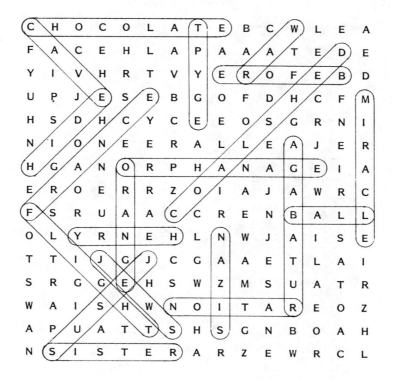

CROSSWORD

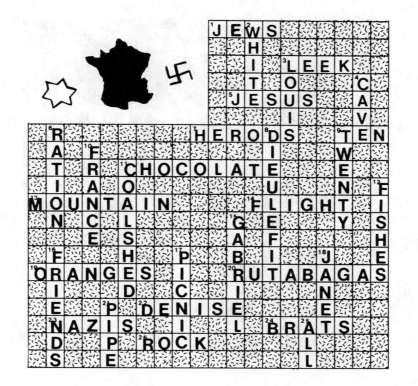

75

The Upstairs Room

By Johanna Reiss

SEEK-A-WORD

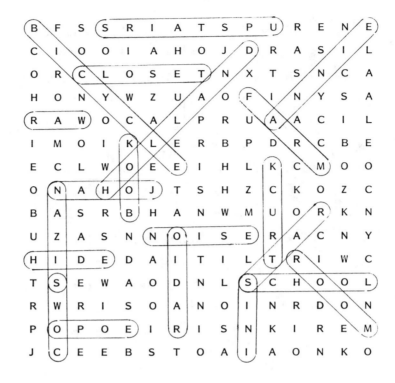

CROSSWORD

The Westing Game

By Ellin Raskin

SEEK-A-WORD

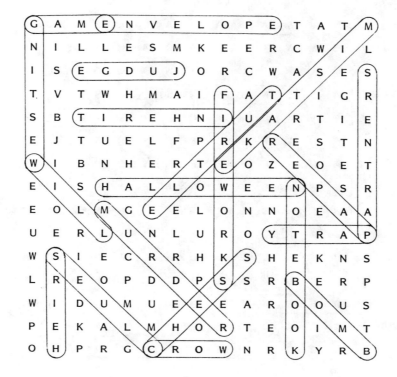

CROSSWORD

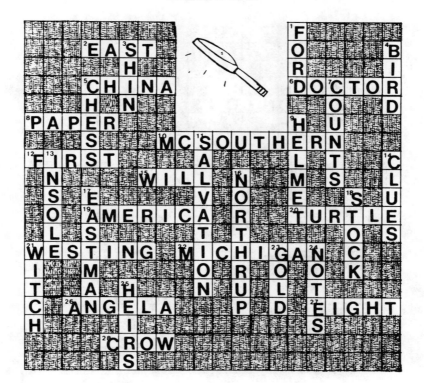

Where the Lilies Bloom

By Bill Cleaver and Vera Cleaver

SEEK-A-WORD

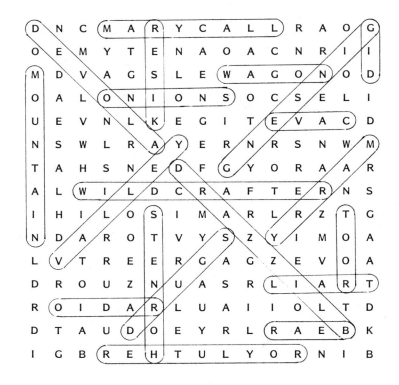

CROSSWORD

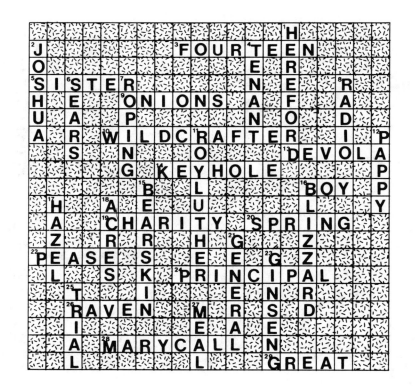

The Witch of Blackbird Pond

By Elizabeth G. Speare

SEEK-A-WORD

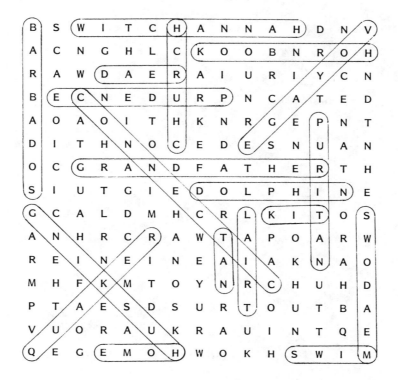

CROSSWORD

79

INDEXES

Index of Recommended Grade Levels
by Puzzle Title

Index of Puzzles by Recommended Grade Levels

BIBLIOGRAPHY

Babbitt, Natalie. *Tuck Everlasting*. Farrar, 1975. Paper edition. Farrar, n.d.

Bishop, Claire H. *Twenty and Ten*. Viking, 1952. Reprint. Peter Smith, 1984. Paper edition. Penguin, n.d.

Blume, Judy. *It's Not the End of the World*. Bradbury, 1972. Paper editions. Bantam, 1981; Dell, 1982.

Burnford, Sheila. *The Incredible Journey*. Little, 1961. Paper edition. Bantam, 1977.

Byars, Betsy. *The Summer of the Swans*. Viking, 1971. Paper edition. Penguin, 1981.

Cleary, Beverly. *Ramona and Her Father*. Morrow, 1977. Paper edition. Dell, n.d.

Cleaver, Bill and Vera Cleaver. *Where the Lilies Bloom*. Lippincott, 1969. Paper edition. NAL, 1974.

De Angeli, Marguerite. *The Door in the Wall*. Doubleday, 1949. Paper edition. Scholastic, 1984.

Fitzhugh, Louise. *Harriet the Spy*. Harper, 1964. Paper edition. Dell, 1978, 1984.

Fleming, Ian. *Chitty Chitty Bang Bang*. Random, 1964. Reprint. Amereon Ltd., 1984.

Forbes, Esther. *Johnny Tremain*. Houghton, 1943. Reprint. Buccaneer Books, 1981. Paper edition. Dell, 1969.

Fox, Paula. *The Slave Dancer*. Bradbury, 1973. Paper edition. Dell, 1975.

Fritz, Jean. *The Cabin Faced West*. Coward, 1958.

George, Jean. *My Side of the Mountain*. Dutton, 1959.

Gipson, Fred. *Old Yeller*. Harper, 1956. Paper edition. Harper, 1964.

Hamilton, Virginia. *M.C. Higgins the Great*. Macmillan, 1974. Paper edition. Dell, 1976.

Lewis, C. S. *The Lion, the Witch, and the Wardrobe*. Macmillan, 1950. Paper edition. Macmillan, 1968.

Norton, Mary. *The Borrowers*. Harcourt, 1953. Paper edition. Harcourt, 1965.

O'Brien, Robert C. *Mrs. Frisby and the Rats of NIMH*. Atheneum, 1971. Paper edition. Atheneum, n.d.

O'Dell, Scott. *The Black Pearl*. Houghton, 1967. Paper edition. Dell, 1977.

Paterson, Katherine. *The Great Gilly Hopkins*. Crowell, 1978. Paper edition. Avon, 1979.

Raskin, Ellin. *The Westing Game*. Dutton, 1978. Paper edition. Avon, 1980.

Reiss, Johanna. *The Upstairs Room*. Crowell, 1972. Paper edition. Bantam, 1973.

Robinson, Barbara. *The Best Christmas Pageant Ever*. Harper, 1972. Paper editions. Avon, 1973; Tyndale, 1982.

Speare, Elizabeth G. *The Witch of Blackbird Pond*. Houghton, 1958. Paper edition. Dell, n.d.